STYLISTICS AND PSYCHOLOGY: Investigations
of Foregrounding

CROOM HELM LINGUISTICS SERIES

CROOM HELM
LINGUISTICS SERIES

Stylistics and Psychology
Investigations of foregrounding

WILLIE VAN PEER

CROOM HELM
London • Sydney • Wolfeboro, New Hampshire

©1986 W. Van Peer
Croom Helm Ltd, Provident House, Burrell Row,
Beckenham, Kent, BR3 1AT
Croom Helm Australia Pty Ltd, Suite 4, 6th Floor,
64-76 Kippax Street, Surry Hills, NSW 2010, Australia

British Library Cataloguing in Publication Data

Peer, Willie van
   Stylistics and psychology: investigations
   of foregrounding.
   1. Language and languages — Style
   2. Structural linguistics
   I. Title
   149'.96 P301
   ISBN 0-7099-2604-9

Croom Helm, 27 South Main Street,
Wolfeboro, New Hampshire 03894-2069, USA

Library of Congress Cataloging-in-Publication Data

Peer, Willie van,
   Stylistics and psychology.

   1. Foregrounding. 2. Criticism. I. Title.
PN226.P43 1986   801'.95   86-13487
ISBN 0-7099-2604-9

Printed and bound in Great Britain
by Billing & Sons Limited, Worcester.

EDITORIAL STATEMENT

CROOM HELM LINGUISTICS SERIES

Chief Editor
Professor John Hawkins, University of Southern California

Consultant Editors
Professor Joseph Aoun, University of Southern California
Professor Bernard Comrie, University of Southern California
Dr Richard Hudson, University College London
Professor James Hurford, University of Edinburgh
Professor Douglas Pulleyblank, University of Southern
  California

The Croom Helm Linguistics Series does not specialise in any one area of language study, nor does it limit itself to any one theoretical approach. Synchronic and diachronic descriptive studies, either syntactic, semantic, phonological or morpho-logical, are welcomed, as are more theoretical 'model-building' studies, and studies in sociolinguistics or psycholinguistics. The criterion for a work's acceptance is the quality of its contribution to the relevant field. All texts published must advance our understanding of the nature of language in areas of substantial interest to major sectors of the linguistic research community. Traditional scholarly standards, such as clarity of presentation, factual and logical soundness of argumentation, and a thorough and reasoned orientation to other relevant work, are also required. Within these indispensable limitations we welcome the submission of creative and original contributions to the study of language.

The editors and publisher wish to draw this series to the attention of scholars, who are invited to submit manuscripts or book-proposals to:

Professor John Hawkins, Department of Linguistics, University of Southern California, Los Angeles, CA 90089-1693, USA: *or to* Jonathan Price, Linguistics Editor, Croom Helm Publishers, Provident House, Burrell Row, Beckenham, Kent BR3 1AT, UK.

CONTENTS

Preface

Preface

This book is essentially a revised version of my Ph.D. dissertation, which was submitted to the Department of Linguistics at the University of Lancaster. There is a sense in which the debts of gratitude incurred during the process of producing such a work cannot be adequately repaid in a 'Preface'. The commentaries and criticisms offered by Geoffrey Leech and by Michael Short during my stay in Lancaster and after have enabled me to improve the quality of the work. I owe them my deep appreciation for their unfaltering support. Similarly, I cannot express enough my gratitude to Mimi Debruyn. Without her help, encouragement and sacrifices in her personal life, this study would not have been possible.

The research has been realized through a scholarship, offered by the British Council, which I hereby gratefully acknowledge.

WvP

Chapter One

THE THEORY OF FOREGROUNDING: THE STATE OF THE ART

INTRODUCTION

This chapter reviews the major contributions made to the theory of foregrounding, from its roots in Russian Formalism, its elaboration in (Prague) Structuralism, to its further development in (British) stylistics. Attention will also be given to the influence of linguistics on the concept, and to its application in actual analyses of literary texts. The chapter concludes with a proposal of what could be called a 'standard' form of the theory.

FORMALISM

As is the case with so many present-day notions in the theory of literature, the notion of foregrounding similarly has its roots in the work of the Russian Formalists. The name most often associated with the concept in this connection, is that of Viktor Šklovskij. The function of art, in his view, is to make people aware of the world in a fresh way. The device whereby this is achieved is <u>defamiliarization,</u> or 'making strange' (Russian 'ostranenie').

> And art exists that one may recover the sensation of life; it exists to make one feel things, to make the stone stony. The purpose of art is to impart the sensation of things as they are perceived and not as they are known. The technique of art is to make objects 'unfamiliar', to make forms difficult, to increase the difficulty and length of perception because the process of perception is an aesthetic end in itself and must be prolonged. (Šklovskij 1917: 12)[1]

Thus Šklovskij's theory of literature is a functional one. The task of the poet is to counteract the routine of the reader's attachment to clichés, stock responses and automatized perception, by cutting the familiar objects and events out of their habitual context and portraying them as if they were seen for the first time, hence bringing about a heightened awareness of the world. Thus Šklovskij opposes automatization to perceptibility. It is the latter quality that the artist strives towards. The effect is density ('faktura'), which hinders ease of communication, hence resulting in retardation: the processes of perception and of comprehension are slowed down. The reader is forced to come to grips with the world of the text in a more strenuous and supposedly more rewarding fashion. The main emphasis in the work of Šklovskij and other Formalists was consequently geared at the devices which may activate these processes when readers are confronted with literary works of art.

This led the Formalists, as their name readily indicates to study literature mainly in its formal aspects. One notices in the whole movement a concentration on the poetic text itself, and they stubbornly refused to be diverted from it; cp. Jameson (1972: 43), Pomorska (1968: 120). This eventually led to a sharper formulation of the concept of foregrounding. Against the oversimplification of their predecessors, the Formalists proposed to conceive of literature in terms of deviance from norms[2]. This idea, originally developed by Šklovskij in his notion of estrangement, was widely accepted in the Formalist ranks, notably by Tomaševskij, Ejxenbaum, Tynjanov, and Jakubinskij; see Erlich

(1965: 183-185; 235; 288-289).

The Formalists were not the first, nor the only ones, to advance such a theory of literature, cp. Erlich (1965: 179-180); Milic (1969: 164); Wellek & Warren (1956: 242). In fact it echoed Aristotle's Poetics[3]: 'the unfamiliarity due to this deviation from normal usages will raise the diction above the commonplace, while the retention of some part of the normal forms will make for clarity.' (Dorsch 1965: 63; my emphasis).

The views of the Formalists are not without problems, though. One concerns their use of terminology. Firstly their technical terms are often near to being synonymous, for instance: perceptibility and palpability, defamiliarization and de-automatization, making strange and deformation. For the systematic compilation of Formalist terminology and the context of their theoretical development, see O'Toole & Shukman (1977).

A more serious problem relates to what exactly the concept of defamiliarization stands for. Šklovskij himself was notoriously un-systematic in his use of terms; compare Schmid (1973), Jameson (1972: 52-53). A term such as 'making strange' or 'defamiliarization', for instance, may refer to two things. On the one hand it is meant to describe properties of the actual text, i.e. the literary devices that can be located in the text itself. On the other hand it points to the effect such devices may have on a reader. These two meanings are in fact blended together in the terms employed by Šklovskij and several other Formalists. This can be understood in the light of their aim to develop a functional theory of literature, where text and reader both have their place. However, such terminological bivalency may easily be missed, as is witnessed by Doležel (1968: 150), who complains that the notion of defamiliarization contains a strong psychological bias, which was even-tually redressed by more linguistically orientated scholars, such as Roman Jakobson.

Evaluating the work of the Russian Formalists, in particular Šklovskij's concept of 'making strange', Wellek & Warren (1956: 242) remark that it lays too much emphasis on the values of novelty and surprise[4], and that it is notably 'relativist'. Wellek (1971: 67) argues, in agreement with Stankiewicz (1960: 70), that poetry need not violate any rules of language and still remain what it is, 'a highly patterned and organized mode of verbal expression'. Jameson (1972: 42-98) adds to this that the broader social functions of literature are not taken into account, and that the theory comes close to being tautological.

Perhaps the most fundamental objection raised by Jameson is of a logical nature. If the concept of defamiliarization is called upon to describe and explain the reception of literary works, then one may wonder what will happen when the reading public becomes conscious (or weary) of 'art as defamiliarization'. Presumably, the pendulum may then swing back, and the concept of defamiliarization becomes self-abolishing. And as Jameson (1972: 91) ironically remarks, if it goes, the entire theory goes with it.

The question is, however, whether readers will ever get tired of defamiliarization as such. A certain remoteness from the habitual does seem to be a fundamental characteristic of art; compare Kreitler & Kreitler (1972: 157-163; 223-224). The device of defamiliarization may profitably be invoked to describe particular aspects of this remoteness in analysing literary works of art.

The Formalists saw the literary text as their prime source of investigation. At the same time they shifted the theoretical attention in the direction of the reader's interaction with the text. It is this concentration on the reception of the poetic text that made possible their formulation of a functional theory of literature, with its bearing on the anthropological study of art; see Schmid (1973: 265). It provided a psychological explanation for the internal organization of the poetic text, for its perception by the reader and a sociological rationale for the dynamics of literary evolution. It is in Jakobson & Tynjanov (1928) - see O'Toole & Shukman, vol. 4 (1977: 49-51) - that one finds a new awareness of literary phenomena which resulted in a model in which most of the earlier dilemmas were resolved. Fokkema (1976: 163) observes that, when they started studying (and stressing) the interdependence of the various elements of literature as opposed to their earlier emphasis on devices in isolation, however, the shift towards structuralism became fact. For further historical treatment of the ideas generated by Russian Formalist theory of literature, see Doležel (1968), Erlich (1965), Flaker & Zmegač (1974), Fokkema (1976).

STRUCTURALISM

The term 'foregrounding' itself was introduced into the study of literature in the West by Garvin (1964), as a translation of the Czech 'aktualisace', employed in the works of several Prague scholars. Just as the Formalists the Prague Structuralists were intrigued by the nature of artistic phenomena and the role they play in human society. At the same time their own aim was to embed such a functional approach in the framework of their structuralist linguistics, which had by that time provided interesting insights and methods. In this perspective Havránek (in Garvin: 1964) develops his argument on the functional differentiation of the standard language. On the basis of three processes (intellectualization, automatization, and foregrounding) Havránek proposes differentiation of a language into three modes[5]: that of scientific language, where the function is accuracy, everyday language, which is geared to conventional communicative purposes, and poetic language, which attracts attention to itself by virtue of the foregrounding devices it contains.

Havránek conceives of this classificatory system as a graded opposition, with scientific language on the one extreme, and the automatisms of everyday language situated in the middle of the scale. At the other extreme one finds poetic language, typically displaying foregrounding devices. This does not imply that everything within poetic language will be foregrounded, because it needs for its very existence the presence of automatized language. The crucial difference however, according to Havránek, between poetic and everyday language, is that the former cannot be limited to automatized language, while the latter usually is. Various criticisms of such distinctions between poetic and everyday language have been proposed; see, for instance, Culler (1975: 161-164), Fish (1973), Pratt (1977). But the fact that the critical discussion around the relationship between literary and non-literary uses of language continues, shows that the issue is still very much alive, and to some extent, unresolved.

Perhaps the most influential figure in shaping the concept of foregrounding has been the Prague scholar Jan Mukařovský. His ideas gradually found their way to the West through other Czech figures, such as René Wellek, F. Vodička, L. Doležel, etc. The major breakthrough came with the publication of Garvin (1964) which contains two seminal articles: Mukařovský (1964a) and (1964b). According to Mukařovský, the essence of poetic language lies in the violations of the norms of the standard language, and this relationship is seen as essential for the very existence of poetry, while at the same time the violations of the standard found in poetry enrich the standard language itself (see Mukařovský: 1964a: 51-54): 'its systematic violation is what makes possible the poetic utilization of language; without this possibility there would be no poetry'. In this sense, Mukařovský takes over the notion already formulated by the Russian Formalists that the very essence of poeticality lies in the deformation of the language, in the violation of its rules. It is interesting to note, however, especially with regard to later approaches in which the two aspects of deviation and parallelism were unified, that Mukařovský also makes some oblique references to parallelism (1977: 23).

As such, poetic language is not defined in terms of its properties, but in terms of its function, which lies in its aesthetic effect. This aesthetic effect results from the fact that attention is concentrated on the linguistic sign itself, and not, as in ordinary language, on the communicative result. In everyday speech, such a concentration on the sign itself would only hamper efficient communication. Hence everyday speech is largely automatized, and any aesthetic effect that may occur, is subordinate to the flow of ideas. Poetic language then draws from the stock furnished by other levels of language, especially the literary varieties of the standard language, which constitute the background against which the linguistic aspects of the work are perceived. Any deviations from the standard language (in its literary form) are evaluated in poetry as artistic devices.

The aim of the poet must consequently lie in achieving the maximum of foregrounding. However, this is not a matter of quantities. Indeed, as Mukařovský argues, 'foregrounding arises from the fact that a given component in some way, more or less conspicuously, deviates from current usage. If, however, all the components of the work laid claim to this difference, it would no longer be different. The simultaneous foregrounding of all the components is therefore unthinkable' (1964b: 65; compare also 1964a: 44). The maximum of foregrounding is defined by Mukařovský as a result of two forces. One of these resides in the relational character of foregrounding, the other in its consistent and systematic character. A tension arises from the structure of the literary work of art, which is seen as a complex yet unified aesthetic structure, defined by the interrelationships between those items that are foregrounded and those elements in the work that remain in the background (1964a: 48; 1964b: 65). Simultaneously the (good) poet will avoid random deviations. Instead he will try to work towards unity of the work by making the foregrounded components point in the same direction. Such systematic foregrounding creates the most powerful aesthetic structure that a poet can hope for.

A result of the relational character of foregrounding, as outlined above, lies in the indivisibility of the literary work of art: (1964b: 66; 1964a: 45). If the structure of the work hinges on the balance between foregrounded elements and their background, any change in this equilibrium will change the entire network of relationships. Mukařovský thus emphasizes the aesthetic effect that is sought by the poet when introducing foregrounding into his writing, or that is experienced by the reader when encountering it. Such instances of foregrounding are seen as a deviation from current usage, be it the usage of the standard language, or the general set of rules tied to the poetic canon of a given historical period. As such foregrounding is the violation of the schematization of an act.

In other places Mukařovský provides further characteristics of foregrounding: its uncommonness and novelty (1964a: 50), its unexpectedness, unusualness and uniqueness (1964a: 53). This idea that literature results from a deviation from current usage squares with the fact that ordinary speech may contain a high amount of foregrounding too, as Mukařovský himself points out. As examples he cites (1964b: 36-39) the language games children play, onomatopoeia, similes and metaphors that are uncommon and individual, invectives, the choice of less common words, the use of foreign words or dialect expressions, and the use of various foregrounding devices in advertising. How then, can foregrounding be the hallmark of literature in general, or poetry in particular? Mukařovský argues that in all these cases foregrounding devices are employed to attract attention to the subject-matter of the communicative situation, while in poetry they are geared towards themselves, i.e. in order to draw attention to the speech event itself.

The essential difference of foregrounding within and outside the field of literature therefore rests with the yardstick that is used to measure the effect of the particular case of foregrounding. Outside literature this yardstick is the set of aesthetic norms that a society provides. Within poetry the yardstick is the degree of integration of foregrounding into the complete structure of the work. Mukařovský (1964b: 32-35) calls this the 'structured' aesthetic, while the occurrence of foregrounding in everyday language is labelled the 'unstructured' aesthetic. The latter works toward the practical, the momentary, while the former tries to achieve permanence and generality (in the sense of being independent of the speaker or of the concrete communicative situation). However, the relationship between the unstructured and the structured aesthetic, as well as that between the standard language and its use in poetry, is not a static one. There is, for one thing, a mutual interpenetration, in that the standard language provides the background against which foregrounding takes place, thereby constraining the kind of language used in poetry. On the other hand, poetic language itself shapes the standard language, as when poetic neologism passes into the standard, or when intonational or syntactic patterns are borrowed from poetic language and introduced into the standard; see Mukařovský (1964a: 50-54). Furthermore, the norm of the standard changes continually, and as this is the background on to which foregrounding is projected, the structure of the work itself, and hence its reception and interpretation may change considerably as time goes by.

As may have become clear from the account of Mukařovský's viewpoints, the notion of foregrounding approaches a critical point when it is employed to distinguish literature from non-literary uses of language, which apparently contains frequent use of foregrounding devices too. Surely the distinction between attracting attention to subject-matter or to the speech event itself is a difficult one to draw. Likewise serious obstacles are involved in disentangling the 'structured' from the 'unstructured' aesthetic, or 'momentary' from 'permanent' effects. Very similar theoretical and methodological problems arise in the work of Roman Jakobson, which will be discussed in the following section.

ROMAN JAKOBSON

In Mukařovský's conception the theory of foregrounding mainly emphasizes distortional aspects of the literary work of art. Starting from a different angle, Roman Jakobson stressed yet another aspect subsumed under the general concept of foregrounding, i.e. that of parallelism. Jakobson starts from what he sees as the elementary factors that constitute any speech event. In order for a communicative act to be successful, he argues, a particular code must establish a contact between two persons, the addresser and the addressee, in such a way that a particular message will refer to a particular context in reality. The nature of any communicative event then, is determined by the amount of emphasis that is placed on each of these six factors. Thus Jakobson distinguishes six different basic functions of language, according to which of the six variables is dominant in the act of communication. This is made possible by the 'set' of the participants in the particular communicative situation. Functional labels that correspond to the dominant factors are provided. If the emphasis is on the addresser, the dominant function is the <u>emotive</u> one; if there is more emphasis on the context, the function is mainly <u>referential</u>; if the speech event has as its main purpose to establish or maintain social contact, the function is of a predominantly <u>phatic</u> nature. The <u>metalingual</u> function is in operation when the utterance is geared towards the code itself. Focus on the addressee causes the <u>conative</u> function to come to the fore. Finally, if the set is towards the message itself, Jakobson speaks of the <u>poetic</u> function. It is characterized by its concentration on the message <u>per se,</u> drawing attention to itself and to its own properties. In this sense, the poetic function of language is self-conscious and auto-referential; see Jakobson (1960: 357).

Although he insists that the poetic function is not confined to poetry and although verbal art may fulfil other functions beside its dominant poetic function, Jakobson claims that the characteristics of the poetic function form the proper subject-matter of literary studies. Hence poetics is considered to be a branch of linguistics, studying one of the major functions of language. The basic characteristic that Jakobson finds in the poetic function lies in the fact that the poetic use of language 'projects the principle of equivalence from the axis of selection into the axis of combination' (1960: 358). In other words, while one would expect <u>different</u> kinds of elements that have been selected at different points in the syntagmatic chain, poetic language typically shows repeated combinations of the <u>same</u> kinds of elements. Although this phenomenon, known as parallelism, occurs in daily language as well, Jakobson argues that in literature it acquires the highest status in the organization of the work of art and that it pervades all other aspects. In the words of Hawkes (1977: 81):

> By the use of complex inter-relationships, by emphasizing resemblances and by promoting through repetition 'equivalences' or 'parallelisms' of sound, stress, image, rhyme, poetry patterns and 'thickens' language, 'foregrounding' its formal qualities, and

consequently 'backgrounding' its capacity for sequential, discursive and referential meaning[6].

Jakobson has provided analyses of literary texts in numerous articles. In most of these the texts treated are fragments of larger texts. See, for instance, Jakobson (1960, 1966, 1968). But in Jakobson and Levi-Strauss (1962) and Jakobson and Jones (1970) the method is aimed at a (short) literary work of art: in the former case a poem by Baudelaire, in the latter a Shakespearian sonnet. The authors set out to provide a 'complete' description of all observable patterning in the poems under study. In this way an impressive categorization is made of the various equivalences on the phonological and grammatical levels of linguistic organization.

The first kind of criticism aimed at Jakobson is of a <u>theoretical</u> nature, and as such takes its place in the discussion of the theory of literary interpretation. The objection is that even a thorough scanning of all instances of parallelism in a poem does not provide a framework for a justifiable interpretation of the patterns that are described, which in themselves are only neutral with regard to interpreting the text. This difficulty can be clearly observed in the actual analyses carried out by Jakobson and his fellow-workers: of the initial groundwork done in the description of equivalences and contrasts, some disappear when it comes to interpretation, obviously because they are not felt to be as salient as others; see, for instance, Short (1973b: 86). It is not clear on what grounds some of the patterns outlined in the preliminary stages of the analyses are later raised to unifying principles of the text, while others disappear from the field of view. Perhaps the clearest wording of this viewpoint is found in Riffaterre (1972: 370), posing the crucial question of <u>relevance:</u> which of the parallelisms are crucial to the interpretation of the poem, which ones are subordinate, and which ones are simply trivial in terms of an interpretation? In Jakobson's approach there is no telling, because the objective inventory of all formal patterns (if this is a real possibility at all) does not open up a window on interpretation. In a similar vein

Shapiro (1976: 68-85) argues that Jakobson's claim must necessarily remain sterile because it does not take into account values, which are inherent qualities in human language. Jakobsonian analysis narrows down the geometricization of linguistic structures to the point where any meaningfulness of the spatial pattern must necessarily disappear. This is, Shapiro argues (1976: 79), because Jakobson's definition of the poetic function 'takes into account not the value of the various elements which are juxtaposed along the syntagmatic axis (contiguity), but rather the mere fact of their being juxtaposed'.

Some critics of Jakobson have concentrated on methodological aspects. Culler (1975: 55-74) takes issue with the implicit claim in Jakobson's analyses that linguistics provides an algorithm for an exhaustive and unbiased description of a text, on the basis of which one can then build an interpretation. The problem with Jakobson's method is that it is at the same time too narrow and too wide in scope. It is too narrow because it yields analyses that are far from complete, in the sense that one can very easily point to patterns in the text that have apparently not been registered by the algorithm. It is too wide because it may also be applied and with very similar results to types of text which are obviously of a non-literary nature. Thus Culler (1975: 63) demonstrates how Jakobson's own writings show the same kind of parallelism as the ones claimed by Jakobson to represent the core of poeticality. Similarly Werth (1976) is able to expose the same kinds of parallelism again, this time in a piece of doggerel verse and in a passage from The Sunday Times. The conclusion to both Culler and Werth is clear: Jakobson's method does not provide a sufficient means to discover the poetical qualities of a text. This does not mean that Jakobson's approach and his particular analyses of poems are thereby rendered nonsensical. In the first place the overall interpretation arrived at by Jakobson does have meaningful insights to offer, and to a rather large extent is agreed upon even by his critics; see Short (1973b: 90). What Jakobson leaves out, however, is the relevance of a particular pattern, i.e. the necessary link between the occurrence of a grammatical or phonological pattern and a particular poetic effect.

Riffaterre (1972: 374) has proposed to study such effects as an alternative to Jakobson's method. In the present study both approaches have been combined, by investigating reader responses (as Riffaterre suggests) in relation to particular instances of parallelism to be found in poetry (as Jakobson has shown). In this way it may be possible to detect those mechanisms that constrain Jakobson's theory sufficiently. What is needed is clearly the 'rules of the literary game' which determine what particular pattern has 'value' in the game and which one has not.

One final point should be made about such following up of Jakobson's study at this point. Jakobson (1960: 356) talks about the set ('Einstellung') towards the message as crucial for the poetic function to become operative. This could be interpreted as meaning that the reader, as a participant in the act of literary communication, is 'set' towards the poetic function. It could therefore be the case that in reading poems people tend to be geared towards the parallelisms, and to find aesthetic reward in them, while they might not adopt such a set when reading prose. At least one psychologist commenting on Jakobson saw this possibility as one of the ways in which the game of poetry works:

> The poet announces, by the form in which he writes it, that his product is a poem; the announcement carries an invitation to consider the sounds of these words as well as their meaning. If we wish to participate in this game, we will adopt an attitude of phonetic, as well as semantic, sensitivity, to the words he uses. (Miller 1960: 390).

As Raeff (1955) has shown, subjects provided quite different associations when they were presented with words in a poetic context from when they were confronted with the same words in a prose context. In the latter case, the properties associated typically related to external qualities of the objects referred to by the words. Within a poetic context however, the associations displayed a clear tendency to be related to the sound of the words themselves. Raeff's findings thus seem to provide confirmation of Jakobson's notion of a special 'set' towards the linguistic sign that individuals in our culture typically adopt when reading literature.

SYNTHESIS: BRITISH STYLISTICS

The previous sections have outlined two stylistic devices, i.e. deviation and parallelism, bringing about foregrounding, which itself is at least in part a psychological phenomenon. The combination of these two forces into a coherent theory was only attempted in the nineteen sixties. Starting from Jakobson's distinction between paradigmatic and syntagmatic relations, Leech (1966) makes a distinction between two types of foregrounding. Paradigmatic foregrounding consists in the selection of an item that is not permitted in the normal range of available choices. The opposite kind of foregrounding depends on the syntagmatic principle: the poet keeps repeating a selected linguistic element at different points in the linear organization of language, where one would under normal conditions expect a variation in the selections made. Hence syntagmatic foregrounding may schematically be represented as follows:

$$A \quad B \quad C \quad D \quad \underset{\uparrow}{D}$$

while paradigmatic foregrounding is of the following form:

$$A \quad B \quad C \quad D \quad \underset{\uparrow}{9}$$

In this way the two principles of foregrounding are combined into one unifying theory. Foregrounding may be due either to devices of a deviational/paradigmatic or of a parallelistic/syntagmatic nature; Leech (1970: 121-122). The principle that unites both is that of selection. In the case of a deviation a writer makes a choice outside a range of choices permitted by the language system, while in the case of parallelism the writer repeatedly makes the same selection. These are opposite processes, complementing each other as alternative forces in the organization of poetic texts.

Concerning the generality of statements that a linguist can bring to the study of foregrounding, Leech introduces the idea that deviation and parallelism are a matter of degree, which for their description need a scale of measurement. Leech (1966: 137-140) proposes one scale of institutional and one of descriptive delicacy. Consequently, adequate descriptions of literary texts are only relevant and useful if they are carried out in the light of comparisons with other varieties of the language. In another article, Leech (1970: 123-124) introduces a perhaps even more powerful interpretational constraint: that of the cohesion of foregrounding. In order to carry aesthetic value, there must be cohesion between deviational and parallel items within the text. If they happen to be isolated instances, they may have little to offer in terms of an overall interpretation of the text. If, however, fore-grounded elements are systematically related to each other, their impact will be powerful enough to seriously constrain the number and kinds of interpretations that may be imposed on parallelism the writer repeatedly makes the same selection. These are opposite processes, complementing each other as alternative forces in the organization of poetic texts.

Concerning the generality of statements that a linguist can bring to the study of foregrounding, Leech introduces the idea that deviation and parallelism are a matter of degree, which for their description need a scale of measurement. Leech (1966: 137-140) proposes one scale of institutional and one of descriptive delicacy. Consequently, adequate descriptions of literary texts are only relevant and useful if they are carried out in the light of comparisons with other varieties of the language. In another article, Leech (1970: 123-124) introduces a perhaps even more powerful interpretational constraint: that of the cohesion of foregrounding. In order to carry aesthetic value, there must be cohesion between deviational and parallel items within the text. If they happen to be isolated instances, they may have little to offer in terms of an overall interpretation of the text. If, however, fore-grounded elements are systematically related to each other, their impact will be powerful enough to seriously constrain the number and kinds of interpretations that may be imposed on to the text, a point elaborated further by Short (1973a). In addition to this notion of cohesion I should like to introduce the concept of a nexus of foregrounding. While cohesion of foregrounding refers to different locations of deviance or parallelism in the linear organization of the text, I suggest that at any one point in this linearity a reader may encounter foregrounding devices on several layers of linguistic structure. Thus, for example, such devices may occur simultaneously on the phonological, grammatical, and semantic level. Other things being equal, such a nodal point will be more foregrounded than the occurrence of deviance or parallelism on only one level of linguistic organization[7] only.

In a similar vein, Halliday (1971: 339-345) distinguishes prominence from foregrounding[8]. The former is defined as deviation or parallelism as such. Thus if a particular line in a poem shows a high density of liquids and nasals, such a recurrence of phonemes constitutes prominency. These features will only be perceived as real fore-grounding, according to Halliday, if they are motivated, for instance by the subject-matter or 'vision' of the text, or by the meaning of the text as a whole. This distinction between prominence and foregrounding, as drawn by Halliday, must be understood as an attempt to solve the problem already encountered by Jakobson, i.e. that the presence of particular linguistic configurations, such as deviance and/or parallelism, is not in itself a guarantee for a reader's experiencing it as relevant to his interpretative process. Hence a distinction is drawn between the linguistic structures on the one hand, and their relevance to this process. According to Jakobson, this relevance depends on the mental and attitudinal 'set' of the reader. The solution adopted by Halliday is still situated within the text: a particular instance of prominence becomes foregrounding if the general meaning of the text provides its foundation.

THE INFLUENCE OF DEVELOPMENTS IN LINGUISTICS

It should be mentioned at this point that the advent of formal grammars in linguistics strongly influenced the approach to deviational devices of foregrounding. The notions of well-formedness and acceptability in generative grammar seemed to stylisticians to provide a ready correspondence to the 'background' against which foregrounding devices operate. If descriptions of such deviations could be embedded into a more rigorous theoretical framework, such as for instance, promised by Chomsky (1964), a firm anchorage for the concept of foregrounding would be provided. Moreover, such an assimilation of insights from generative grammar could offer an interesting outlook on the actual interpretation of a deviant string by readers, by outlining the shortest route back to the grammatical string as the most natural way to interpret deviant utterances; see for instance Katz (1964), Ziff (1964), Fowler (1971: 238-248), Weinreich (1972). For a discussion of these views, see Lipski (1977). Thorne (1970) is to be interpreted within this evolution, as is Levin (1964).

Also within this framework, Levin (1965: 226) has argued for a distinction between _external_ and _internal_ deviation. The former violates a norm or a rule that lies outside the limits of the poem itself: the grammar of the language, the conventional norms for writing poetry, the traditional subject-matter of poems, the cultural and aesthetic norms of a given society, etc. The latter form is described as a departure from a norm that is set up within the boundaries of the poetic text. As such internal deviation occurs against the background of the remainder of the text itself. Most stylisticians would agree on the importance of internal deviation as a foregrounding device. Nevertheless the situation is somewhat discouraging, as its analyses are rarely, if ever, combined into a general approach to the phenomenon. A difficult question in this respect is how to generalize about internal deviations beyond each individual text. How, in other words, can one develop a more systematic description of the device? As yet, no such enterprise has been undertaken, and the notion stands in all its generality as an obvious, but little understood, technique that poets have developed.

In an earlier article, Levin (1963) had already distinguished between two kinds of external deviation: determinate and statistical deviation. The first of these has already been referred to. It is the kind of deviation that results from the breaking of a rule, e.g. the violation of a linguistic rule, or the clear infringement of an established cultural code. But one often encounters in poetry a kind of deviation that is the result of 'rarity'. In such cases the string is not really deviant but only highly unexpected. In other words, by using an element in a context where its probability of occurrence is low, attention is drawn to this unexpected element. Hence a crucial concept for the description of statistical deviation is that of context[9]. The 'rare' element may go completely unnoticed in another context. This has an important consequence: a comparison with the language as a whole will be necessary, but this time the operation will involve some kind of quantification[10]. However, it must be clear from previous argumentation that it is not the frequencies of occurrence which are crucially important, but the relationship of such probabilities to the specific context in which they can be observed. Thus statistical data can only tell us part of the importance of a particular pattern or prominency; its relevance in the total organization of the work cannot be revealed by numerical data alone; the study of foregrounding must include other factors as well.

The competence of a native speaker includes knowledge of how and when to use certain meaning-carrying units. One could call these the 'rhetorical' rules of the language, and they can be studied for their own sake, as is witnessed by the recent growth in the study of pragmatics; cp. Leech (1983), Levinson (1983). It is to this field that a number of authors have taken recourse in the hope of finding some hints on how to solve the problem of the functioning of deviance in poetry. As Austin (1962) and Searle (1969) have shown, communicative acts are governed by speech act conditions. But, as Austin (1962: 9) remarks, these do not apply to non-serious language use, and poetry is considered as such, thereby escaping the normal felicity conditions of everyday language. Thus for Ohmann (1971) the issue is that a poem, by violating the rhetorical conventions, suspends the normal felicity conditions of everyday communication. The result is not communicative failure, but a new and special kind of relationship between language and participants. Similarly Widdowson (1972), (1975) has argued that all poetry is deviant from a communicative point of view, which may, but does not necessarily, entail the use of ungrammatical language. Pragmatic deviance, according to Widdowson, lies in the fact that the author cannot be identified with the addresser in the literary text. Pratt (1977), making use of Grice's Cooperative Principle discusses the exploitation by poets of conversational implicatures.

THE ANALYSIS OF FOREGROUNDING IN LITERARY TEXTS

So far the emphasis has been on theoretical aspects of foregrounding. However, for any stylistic theory its practical applicability in the analysis of actual texts is of high importance too. The usefulness of the concept of foregrounding has so far been demonstrated in the study of a large and varied sample of literary fragments. It is in the more detailed stylistic analysis of complete texts however, that the theory of foregrounding is put to a more severe test. Here again the historical and generic variation is rather wide: English, but also Slavonic studies (in the works of Formalists and Structuralists) are present. Add to this Jakobson's study of Baudelaire and of Portuguese poetry (in Bann & Bowlt 1972: 20-25), and the large scale study by Groos (1975) of the Rabelaisian narrative, and Romance studies seem to be fairly represented as well.

General theories of literature should preferably also be applicable to literary works that are not part of the Western middle- and upper-class canon of 'valuable' works. A number of studies have been carried out to investigate foregrounding in such texts. Jakobson (1960) contains references to Serbian, Chinese, and American Indian poetry; Cluysenaar (1976) analyses a medieval carol, and Leech (1969) refers to biblical fragments and their Swahili translations. At the same time several contributions to the study of folklore were made by both the Russian Formalists and the Structuralists; see for instance, O'Toole & Shukman, (vol. 4, 1977: 4), Bann & Bowlt (1972: 48-72), Erlich (1965: 204-206 and 249-250). Moser (1974) studied foregrounding devices in the Mande epic, an oral poem from the Mande region in present-day Mali, dating back to about the 13th century. A tape-recorded delivery of the epic by one of the bards of the Mande region was used for analysis. Moser reports that the oral epic contains a high number of devices that are typical for foregrounding as they have been treated in the theoretical literature.

From this short review it is clear that the theory of foregrounding has been applied to the study of a wide body of literary texts: poetry and prose, old and new, western and oriental. Hence the framework it presents to the student of literature is potentially advantageous, in that it is both a general and flexible one. The theory of foregrounding therefore seems to offer an interesting starting-point for further development. Recent attempts at an integration of the various strands in the theory also allow for the conceptualization of some kind of standard formulation of the theory. Summarizing the main points of this chapter I now wish, by way of a conclusion, to outline such a standard version of the theory of foregrounding. The aim of this exercise cannot, of course, be standardization alone. As a result of it, we may, it is hoped, sharpen our perception of the theory itself.

INTEGRATION: THE THEORY OF FOREGROUNDING

Foregrounding then, is to be understood as a pragmatic concept, referring to the dynamic interaction between author, (literary) text and reader. On the one hand, the material presence of certain foregrounding devices will guide the reader in his interpretation and evaluation of the text; on the other hand the reader will look for such devices in order to satisfy his aesthetic needs in reading a literary text.

The concept itself derives from an analogy with a fundamental characteristic of human perception, i.e. the necessity to distinguish, in the act of perceiving, a _figure_ against a _ground_ - see, for instance, Vernon (1975: 41-45) - a distinction which has been shown to function aesthetically in the visual arts; see Arnheim (1954), (1971).

Within the interpretation of literature, the term foregrounding is analogous to the _figure_ of perceptual processes, referring to the field of tension between what the reader experiences as being the foreground of the text on the one hand, and whatever aspects of the text he perceives as being more in the background. As such the theory of foregrounding refers to a construction principle in the act of interpretation, bearing on processes which are intimately tied to the social psychology of textual interpretation. Within this field of tension it is not the foreground or background as such which is of importance, but the relationship between them, as it is continually being constructed by the reader.

At the same time, the concept of foregrounding may be viewed from the position of the author. The assumption behind it is that authors will in some way or other aim at some kind of influence on the reader. Consequently, they will search for particular means to achieve this aim. The most evident means a writer has at his disposal is the text itself. It may therefore be expected that writers will not merely leave it to chance which kinds of foreground/background-constructions the reader will make. In other words, authors may, while writing, exert control: they may set out marks in the text which will guide the reader into a particular direction of interpretation. The result of this process of exerting control by the author, as well as the construction of a foreground/background tension in the reader's interpretation, becomes manifest through the medium of the text. On the basis of the text as object, i.e. as a linguistic materialization of individual and/or social aims, an interaction process between author and reader(s) comes into being. Because author and reader have, unlike in everyday communication, no direct access to each other, the process of literary interaction is fundamentally indirect in nature. This characteristic has important consequences for the requirements made to the text. One of the possibilities in this respect lies in the creation of a field of tension between foreground and background, as constructed by the writer, and as re-constructed by the reader. Since the nature of the interaction process between writer and reader is indirect, all kinds of factors may negatively influence the level of achievement that is hoped for. Indeed severe mismatches may emerge between what the reader (re)constructs as foreground and background, and what had been aimed at by the author. Thereby different (groups of) readers may also display marked differences between the kind of relationships they perceive between their constructed foreground and background in the text. Generally, however, there will be serious (sub)cultural constraints on the range and quality of interpretations readers may produce. The devices of foregrounding contribute to (culturally and historically) restrain the number and kind of interpretations readers may engage in when confronting a literary text.

Generally, two such devices have been described in the literature as complementary forces: deviation and parallelism. The former refers to a selection of a linguistic item outside the range of normally allowed selections. Three different types of deviation may be distinguished. The first one, internal deviation, is the violation of a norm set up by the text itself. External deviation, however, occurs against the background of a norm outside the text itself. Determinate deviation belongs to this type, and is constituted by a departure from a rule or convention. Such rules and conventions may be of a linguistic, literary, social, cultural, or other kind, but in all cases it must be possible to account for the departure in terms of an infringement of a rule that can be made explicit. This is not the case with statistical deviation, which must be understood as a departure, not from an absolute, but from a relative norm, i.e. one that should be described in terms of probabilities. Thus with statistical deviation no restrictions of a particular code have been infringed, but the case still evokes surprise, depending in its effects on the probabilities with which the norm usually is encountered in a specific context.

The second device by which foregrounding processes may become operative is that of parallelism. This is a pattern of equivalences and/or contrasts that are superimposed on the normal patterns of language organization. While deviance is the result of a choice the poet has made outside the permitted range of potential selections, parallelism is the opposite process, in which the author has repeatedly made the same, or similar, choices where the normal flux of language would tend to variation in selection.

Each of these devices, deviation (with its three different types) and parallelism, may occur on each of the different levels of linguistic organization: phonology, grammar, and semantics. In this way twelve different kinds of foregrounding cases may be observed, i.e. four devices (deviations of an internal, determinate or statistical kind, plus parallelism) operating on three different language layers (phonology, grammar, semantics).

Furthermore, it is assumed that these devices will gain in impact proportionally to their density and their cohesion. The latter is described as the similarities between individual cases of foregrounding. These may be related to each other or to the text in its entirety, including its thematic structure. As such, cohesion can be considered as a horizontal force in the organization of the text: throughout the linear structure of the text a series of devices may be observed, displaying a number of similarities, thereby working in the same direction, and constraining the number of interpretative possibilities. Density is the opposite force, referring to the vertical compaction of foregrounding devices in the texture of the poem at one particular point. This is achieved by the simultaneous occurrence of foregrounding devices on different linguistic levels, thus creating a nexus of foregrounding at one or more points in the text. Such nodal points will, in cooperation with the principle of cohesion, form a central focus through which the interpretative and evaluative operations of the reader are shaped. For matters of clarity and convenience, the principal ingredients of the standard form of the theory of foregrounding are cast into a summarizing table:

Table 1.1. Linguistic structure of foregrounding

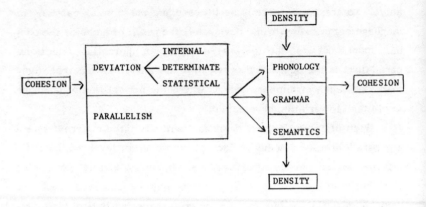

Notes

1. Šklovskij in Lemon & Reis (1965: 12). Note, by the way, that the word 'technique' in the English title (Art as Technique) already incorporates a particular view: Russian 'priĕm' may also be translated as receiving, reception. This may have some slight effect on the framework in which Šklovskij's claim about defamiliarization is judged by Western scholars.

2. It should be emphasized that from the very beginning the notion of parallelism was also referred to as a literary device, often side by side with defamiliarization. See, for instance, Šklovskij's influential article in Lemon & Reis (1965: 21), Tomasevskij in O'Toole & Shukman (1978: 76-77), and Brik's and Ejxenbaum's articles, discussed in Erlich (1965: 220-223). However, the integration of these two devices was not aimed at by the Formalists. Nor was it, as a matter of fact, achieved by the Prague Structuralists.

3. Not surprisingly, Aristotle is paraphrased by Šklovskij. See Lemon & Reis (1965: 22).

4. See also Wellek (1960: 415, 417-418).

5. In fact Havránek proposes a classification with four different modes. Close examination reveals that the second function, labelled 'workaday technical', is smuggled in obliquely, and is in fact a hybrid form between conversational and scientific uses of the language.

6. On the notion of parallelism, see also Austerlitz (1961), Lotman (1976: 88-89), and Jakobson (1966). Levin (1962) also makes use of a similar concept, under the name 'coupling'.

7. In an embryonic form this idea was already present in Leech (1969: 65): 'What factors enter into the assessment of how strong a parallelism is: whether it extends to both lexical and grammatical choices; whether it operates simultaneously on different layers of structure; whether it involves patterning on both phonological and formal levels.' See also Halliday (1971: 359-360) Hymes (1960).

8. Note that the term 'foregrounding' is also used by Halliday in a purely linguistic sense, indicating 'marked' features, as opposed to 'unmarked' ones; see for instance, Kress (1976: 181). The use of the term by Halliday could also be compared to Chafe (1972). Chafe and Halliday seem to take opposite stands in the sense they ascribe to the term 'foreground'. To Halliday this is something that is 'marked', while for Chafe it implies things that are given, and therefore, 'unmarked'.

9. On implications of context, see also Leech (1969: 183-201), Leech (1970: 126-128), Riffaterre (1960) and Riffaterre (1964), who proposes to replace the concept of 'norm' by 'context' as a more workable notion to describe deviation.

10. It may be interesting to note that Mukařovský (1977: 48) had come to a similar conclusion, when claiming that not only 'marked' sentences, but also an excessive use of 'unmarked' sentence types could serve aesthetic purposes. See also Halliday (1971: 340-344) who argues, however, that there is no clear delimitation between what we have termed 'determinate' and 'statistical' deviation.

Chapter Two

DESIGN OF VALIDATION PROCEDURES

INTRODUCTION

As will have become evident from the previous chapter, the theory of foregrounding, although intuitively appealing, is still rather speculative and on the whole rests on inconclusive evidence. The next step in the present study therefore was to investigate the validity of its claims in formal experiments. It should be remembered that suggestions in that direction have been made: e.g. Fish (1970), Kintgen (1977) and Riffaterre (1959), (1960). However, the experimental design of these proposals has generally been rather loose, and subsequent analyses based on these approaches could only work with rough indications rather than with statistical techniques. More importantly, there is little clarity in these works on the experimental conditions, or on the dependent and independent variables. In the present study, therefore, a more rigorous approach to the problem was attempted. Basically the technique consisted in comparing readers' reactions to a poem they had read with a set of prior predictions, based on the analysis of foregrounding in the poem. This chapter discusses the empirical tests of the theory. The following chapter will concentrate on the way the concrete predictions were derived from the analyses of the poems.

STATEMENT OF THE PROBLEM

The four initial postulates

The first stage in the design of empirical tests consisted in trying to derive a number of empirical variables from the theory. This was not an easy matter in itself and consisted mainly in postulating variables that could be used as parameters of foregrounding in literary texts. Four such initial variables were proposed: memorability, strikingness, importance, and discussion value. Each of these will be discussed in turn.

Memorability. The 'Von Restorff effect'[1] seemed to offer a ready parallel to foregrounding effects. According to this theory words written in another colour, or printed in a different type, or deviating from the normal way of presentation in a text, are easier to remember (at the expense of the surrounding words). It seemed plausible that a corresponding effect might take place in poetry. A passage that is foregrounded differs from its context in a somewhat similar way as the words printed in a different way in the von Restorff experiments. It was therefore hypothesized that foregrounded passages of a text would be recalled by informants with a significantly higher frequency than the parts of the text that a stylistic analysis would describe as forming the background of the text. Hence the theory of foregrounding would predict that when presented with a free recall task, subjects (henceforward Ss) will remember items from the foreground (henceforward FG) correctly more often than those from the background (henceforward BG), and the degree of difference in Ss' performance in recalling items from these two sets will be statistically significant.

Strikingness. From the earliest formulations of the theory it has been stressed that foregrounding may be characterized by its strikingness: what is in the 'foreground', what is de-familiarized or de-automatized, what is 'made strange', etc. will generally strike the reader. It was therefore assumed that a blanket term such as strikingness would correspond to the main dimensions of FG as described in the literature. What is foregrounded is striking, unexpected, surprising, unusual, etc. It was decided to employ a rather neutral term such as 'striking' (instead of 'significant', 'unusual', 'strange', 'unfamiliar', 'novel', etc.), on the basis of the fact that a neutral term is more accessible to a range of informants and at the same time may be less parasitic on personal value systems than terms such as 'strange', 'weird', etc. 'Striking' at the same time preserves the foremost quality of FG discussed in the literature and still allows informants a genuine degree of subjectivity in response, in the sense that most people will not think that there are fixed external standards for 'strikingness'. Hence if Ss are asked to indicate those passages in a text they feel to be most striking, they will, according to predictions made by the theory, indicate passages that belong to the FG of the text rather than BG-passages, and the difference between both classes will be significant in statistical terms.

Importance. Relevant as the semi-affective postulate of strikingness may be, this notion should be complemented by a more cognitively oriented measure. In order to investigate the way in which FG contributes to the overall interpretation of a text, the parameter of importance was introduced. It is assumed that elements in the FG (by being most readily perceived) should be most prominent in the interpretation of the text. This assumption was tested by inspecting informants' reaction to the quality of 'importance'. If the theory of FG is in any sense correct, one would expect readers to indicate FG passages of a text as more 'important' than others. Thus, if one draws up a hierarchy of FG features of a particular text, an arrangement of items along a continuum representing the degree of FG must somehow correspond to a reader's perception of importance. Hence the theory predicts that Ss to a large extent agree on rankings along a scale of 'importance' allocated to different parts of a text, and that their average rankings correspond to the hierarchy of FG elements captured by a stylistic analysis of the text.

As for 'strikingness' it was decided to leave the notion of 'importance' undefined for the subjects in the experiment, on the ground that explanation might introduce other variables, some of which might impose unforeseen demands on the informants that they might identify and subsequently attempt to meet. Consequently the qualities of strikingness and importance were presented in the experiment without any elucidation whatsoever. To make up for any deficiencies in leaving such crucial terms unspecified, the fourth variable was developed.

Discussion value. This variable refers to the fact that in a particular situation people will tend to agree to a large extent which passages of a poem are most worthy of comment, discussion, explanation or analysis. The theory of foregrounding would then claim that informants would agree on a high 'discussion-value' for FG parts, and a low one for items belonging to the BG of the text. In this part of the experiment as much relevant pragmatic knowledge was introduced into the experimental setting as was possible within the constraints setting up a test situation. A social situation was described to the subjects: they had to pretend to be teachers of English to 17-year olds. Assuming that all the children in their class had understood all the lexical items in the poem, which passages would they, the teachers, propose for explanation, discussion, comment, etc.

A problem of test instruments

With these four postulates in mind one could design specific experiments. However, in stylistics the situation is quite different from other social sciences, where test instruments have been in use for a long time, and where serious investigation has been made into both the validity and reliability of the instruments. In the present situation, test instruments had to be designed, but the scope of the study did not allow for an extensive investigation of either validity or reliability of these instruments. From this situation arises the basic paradox of this empirical study: it was not known whether the theoretical model under examination was correct, while at the same time it was not, as yet, known whether the test instruments developed to find a decisive answer to the first question, were themselves accurate or appropriate. A corollary of this was that any negative results obtained in such experiments could not be readily interpreted. The theory might be wrong or the data-gathering methods might not be adapted to the purpose of the investigation. However, and this is a crucial aspect to be stressed, although negative results could not be attributed to a specific cause, positive results would be significant for the theory. Indeed, although in principle it is possible that inappropriate test instruments may provide positive results, the chances that such may occur for different subgroups, and in different experiments, are extremely low. Moreover, the probability of wrong test instruments yielding positive results can be calculated in a simple and straightforward way: a design in which the level of significance is set at p   .05 will yield approximately 5% positive results caused by chance fluctuations. Thus replicating the results of one experiment under different test-conditions may provide more powerful evidence in favour of the theory.

Yet another procedural safeguard was taken to prevent our efforts leading us astray. It is noticeable that the four postulates to a certain degree highlight different aspects of the mental operations involved in the processing of foregrounding devices. In order to over-come the problems concerning the test instruments, it was decided to approach the phenomenon of foregrounding from slightly different angles. Thus, by repeated sampling an attempt was made to replicate earlier results and refine predictions while going along, thereby depending on several measures related to the theoretical construct in a meaningful way. This is by no means an unusual procedure in the social sciences:

> 'Most students today would agree that it is appropriate to draw simultaneously on multiple measures of the same attribute or construct - multiple measures hypothesized to overlap in theoretically relevant components, but which do not overlap on measurement errors specific to individual methods.' (Anastasi 1966: 34).

The experimental conditions[2]

These hinge on the <u>dependent variable</u> (DV) and <u>independent variable</u> (IV) respectively. The IV consisted of the poems presented to readers in the experiment, while the DV is formed by the response of these readers to particular tasks we set them. In other words, the IV consists of the text stimuli, appearing under two different conditions: FG or BG, or arranged along a cline from FG to BG. Since we masked our aims in the experiments deliberately, it may be assumed that informants were generally not aware of the two conditions under which the IV appeared. A detailed discussion of the IV is to be found in the following chapter, where the FG/BG-structure of the texts will be closely inspected. The DV was gauged through a number of measures which did not impose high demands on the informants' verbal skills, so as to avoid introducing the factor of linguistic competence, as experimentally demonstrated to determine the response to poetry by Hansson (1964). Instead subjects were offered the constructs for response by the experimenter. This introduces a danger of representing constructs that are not relevant to the problem being investigated. It should be emphasized however, that working with a number of different constructs being used in different test-situations diminishes this danger considerably. Hence the variety in constructs was not merely allowed for, but instead was explicitly aimed at in order not to undermine the validity of the experiments.

To sum up, possibilities of validation for the theory of foregrounding were explored by testing four postulates in experimental conditions. These postulates were associated with four parameters of foregrounding: memorability, strikingness, importance, and discussion value. These were observable in the DV, which consisted of answers elicited from subjects in the tests. The IV under consideration consisted of a sample of poetry, supposedly containing FG. The IV had two values: FG and BG. These then were the two experimental conditions tested when we examined Ss' test-performance. More specifically, it is predicted that the four parameters would be observable in test results in a higher degree when the experimental condition of FG is present than when the condition of BG holds.

Other factors interfering with the design

Individuality. Related to the previous variables is the assumption that the responses of readers to literature are not purely subjective, as is sometimes assumed in literary criticism.[3] The theory of foregrounding does not deny the subjectivity of the literary experience. Yet at the same time it draws attention to the fact that the literary response is by no means arbitrary. Both language and culture impose constraints on the reader's responses. The over-emphasis on the subjective nature of the literary response has led to a relative neglect of the general nature of literary response. Such neglect of generalities is irrational. Instead a rational study of literary response should concentrate on the common features between individual responses, rather than on idiosyncratic aspects, in the same way that medicine recognizes the uniqueness of every single body, but yet concentrates on general patterns which can be established in the study of human health. Because the theory of foregrounding assumes a general pattern in literary response, it was judged necessary to embody this assumption in experimental hypotheses.

Cohesion of foregrounding. Since, as Leech (1970: 123-125) and Mukařovský (1964a: 44) point out, FG operates in a cohesive and systematic way, its contribution to the interpretation of a text must be higher than that of the BG. If the effects of FG are not random but instead operate together in a coherent fashion, then it follows that they will act as signposts for the interpretation of the text. It is therefore to be expected that FG stretches of a text will be experienced as contributing more to the building of an interpretation than will be the case for BG passages of the same text. By asking informants what parts of the text contribute most to their interpretation of the text, confirmation of the systematic nature of FG devices in poetry was sought. At the same time however, this postulate examines the relationship between FG and thematic structure. Since, as has been argued in the previous chapter, foregrounding (as distinct from Halliday's prominence) is related to thematic structure, it will be useful to examine this relationship separately.

Repeated exposure. In a similar vein yet another relationship between FG and interpretative activities may be postulated. Much of the initial impact of powerful FG may be puzzlement for the reader. But, as was stressed in the previous section, the various instances of FG are not diffuse or random. To the degree that they work in the same direction, with repeated exposure to one and the same poem, the consensus of reactions of informants may rise, even if they have had no possibilities of exchanging opinions on them. Since FG is assumed to work in a coherent way, it seems likely that after its initial impact it will lead readers to similar interpretations of the text. If this is so, then it will be observable in that initial responses to FG stretches will be more varied (more idiosyncratic, one could also say) than is the case after repeated exposure to the texts.

The variety in the sample. For the benefit of a rigorous investigation one has to test the predictions for the different postulates with different samples, both of texts and of informants. For a detailed discussion of the sample of informants, see further in this chapter; for a description of the sample of texts, see Chapter 3.

Familiarity with the concept. A matter which stands in need of clarification is the question as to whether an informant's familiarity with the concept of FG will influence his performance in the experiment. If FG is to be taken, not as a mere abstract construction of stylistics, but as a general process that is observable in reality, it cannot be expected that subjects familiar with the theory will respond in a basically different way from subjects who are unaware of the notion of FG. Therefore, if the role played by familiarity with the theory in readers' responses is a minor one then this would give strong support to the generality of the theory as a model for the apperception of literary texts. Although this may appear premature in the present stage of knowledge it may be pointed out that such a claim may indeed be derived from the theoretical literature on foregrounding. (This follows from the functional nature of the theory.) Naturally, such a claim is highly speculative. But by deriving a specific hypothesis from it, i.e. that its generality can be demonstrated by examining the responses of both naive and expert subjects, the claim becomes testable. For this reason some of the experiments were designed to work with subjects who had no prior knowledge of the theory and with subjects who were familiar with it. Their responses were analysed separately, and then compared.

Prior literary training. Since FG is considered by the theory as intimately tied to the function of literature, it may also be expected that a reader's response to it will not be parasitic on the amount of specific literary training received. Thus differences in performance between subjects with respect to this dimension should not be qualitative, but rather of a quantitative nature. In other words, Ss with prior literary training will not perceive other words or passages from a text as FG when compared to other Ss, but it may be that the degree to which they indicate preference or effects will differ. To test this assumption, it was decided to include in the sample of informants individuals who had prior literary training but were not familiar with the theory of foregrounding. As a control group individuals who were completely naive both with respect to the theory of FG and more traditional methods of literary analysis were selected.

Attitudes to poetry. The previous postulate was concerned with the formal education informants had received in matters of literary analysis and discussion. However, it may be the case that responses in experiments may be influenced, not so much by the training subjects had received, but by the attitudes they hold towards the reading of poetry. Therefore an attitude test of the informants taken just before the experiment (giving a profile of subjects' motivational structure towards poetry) was judged to be a necessary complement to the previous hypotheses. A classification of informants along their performance on such an attitude test may reveal whether attitudes influenced responses to FG.

TEST INSTRUMENTS USED

In the previous sections four variables of FG were discussed. Seven other factors were outlined that needed control. Test instruments were then needed to examine the claims the theory makes with regard to these variables. For some of these, no special measuring instruments needed to be developed. This was the case for the variables of individuality, repeated exposure, variety in the sample, familiarity with the concept and prior literary training, as these were studied through comparison of the results of different subgroups in the sample. However, for the remaining factors outlined above, in view of the 'serious shortage of suitable and sophisticated methodologies with which to empirically investigate literary materials' (Lindauer 1974: 178), new test instruments had to be developed. This was the case for each of the four initial variables, and a different part of the experiment was set up for each of these accordingly. They are described in turn below.

The memory test

The first new instrument was designed to test the parameter of 'memorability'. To this end, informants were presented with a short lyrical poem and were asked to read it carefully twice. They were then told to turn over the poem and were presented with a version of the poem in which a number of words had been deleted. This was a kind of cloze-test, but the deletion had not been done in the usual way, i.e. by deleting every n-th word. Instead care had been taken to delete an approximately equal number of words over which there was little doubt as to their status in de FG/BG dichotomy. Ss were then asked to try and fill in the blanks and try to reconstruct the original poem they had just read. The number of right and wrong responses could then be taken as a measure of the memorability of the items. In the framework of the theory of FG, it would be legitimate to expect that FG expressions would be recalled correctly with a higher frequency than those occurring in BG phrases. To put it in more conventional terms: the null-hypothesis (H_0), referring to the fact that the IV had no effect upon the DV, specifies that all items will be recalled with equal frequency; the alternative hypothesis (H_a), assuming that such an effect of the IV on the DV may be expected, states that:

(1) FG items will be recalled correctly more frequently than BG items;

(2) the difference in recall between FG and BG items will be significant.

At the same time, especially as it was not known how such a test would work in practice, a second memory test was conceived of. In this case, Ss were asked, after a concentrated reading of the poem, to write down any (and as many as possible) word(s) they could recall. This test was administered in the pilot testing, with very diffuse results. For this reason it was not repeated in later experiments[4].

The underlining test

Both the variables of 'strikingness' and of 'discussion value' were measured through a simple test in which subjects, after having read the poem, were asked to underline those parts of the text that they found most 'striking' (for the strikingness postulate) or that they considered most worthy of comment, analysis, discussion, etc. if they were teachers of English teaching the poem in class (thus measuring the discussion value). No further explanation was given as to what was meant by 'striking', and no limit was put on the number of items Ss were allowed to underline. They were told they could consider single words, phrases, clauses or sentences as parts to underline. In this case H_0 claims that, since responses to poetry may be highly idiosyncratic, Ss' underlining of what they find 'striking' is random; hence all words or phrases will be underlined with more or less equal frequency. H_a specifies that Ss will underline FG passages more than BG ones, and to such an extent that statistical analysis of the observed differences will yield significant results. In the case of the fourth variable, that of 'discussion value', H_0 specifies that the decisions are random and all items have an equal appeal, whereas H_a claims that FG items play a considerably more important role in this process than BG ones. And the difference in total number of underlinings for the two categories, i.e. FG and BG, will be significant in statistical terms.

The ranking test

In order to investigate the postulates of importance and cohesion, a ranking test was developed. Informants were (after reading time) presented either with fragments from the poem or with different verse-lines, some FG and some BG, while some others were in between these two extremes. They were then asked to rank order these fragments or lines according to the degree of importance they held in the poem. This was done by writing a number to the left of each phrase, a number 1 for the item they held to be the most important one, number 2 for the item coming next, and so on until all the items were assigned a number. H_0 in this case claims that Ss' rankings would be carried out randomly, while H_a predicts Ss to agree considerably in their rankings, to such a degree even that the average ranks agree with predictions derived from the theory of FG, i.e. FG items being ranked as most important and BG ones as least important.

The postulate about the contribution of FG to the interpretation of the text was also tested separately. Informants were presented with a poem to read. Next they were asked to rank order the verse-lines according to their contribution to the overall interpretation of the text. Ranking was carried out in the same way as in the 'importance' test. H_a predicts that considerable agreement among subjects will be found, and that the average ranking will correspond significantly to the predicted ranks, while H_o predicts no such agreement of correspondence to occur in Ss' responses.

The Likert scale

In order to investigate the attitudes informants held towards poetry, a type of questionnaire generally known in the social sciences as the Likert scale was used[5]. A number of statements referring to specific attitudes towards poetry were drawn up and presented to the informants, who were asked to indicate their measure of agreement or disagreement with the statements. The scales employed were of the conventional type, using five points, ranging from extreme agreement to extreme disagreement, with a neutral point in the middle. The major advantage of the Likert scale is that it is easy to develop and administer, while it has been shown to possess a high reliability: see Oppenheim (1966: 140).

Prior to the experiment Ss were presented with such an attitude list and the accompanying scales designed to measure their involvement with poetry. When all results from experiments were obtained they were analysed both with respect to their sampling on the basis of their training, as discussed before, and on the basis of their response to this attitude list.

To summarize then, five different experiments were set up, each of which tested one of the eleven postulates discussed in the previous sections. The remaining postulates were examined by controlling the composition of subgroups in the sample of informants. The tests were labelled with symbols, in the order in which they were developed (and administered). Thus the Likert scale, which was administered prior to all other tests, was called Part A. The memorability test was called part $\underline{B}$, the strikingness test was Part $\underline{C}$, the importance test Part $\underline{D}$; the testing of the discussion value was carried out in Part $\underline{E}$ and finally, the contribution offered to an interpretation of the text by FG configurations took place in part $\underline{F}$.

For ease of exposition, the various tests carried out are here summarized in a table:

Table 2.1. Experiments and test instruments

Variable tested	Test instrument	Experiment
Attitudes to poetry	Likert scale	Part A
Memorability	Cloze-test	Part B
Strikingness	Underlining test	Part C
Importance	Ranking test	Part D
Discussion value	Underlining test	Part E
Cohesion of FG/contribution to interpretation	Underlining test/ Ranking test	Part F

For further inspection a sample of the tests, in the form in which they were presented to the informants, may be consulted in Appendix 1.

THE HYPOTHESES

The previous sections have already outlined the specific experiments to be run and the particular postulates to be tested in them. The discussion of the hypotheses can therefore be brief if we bear in mind what has been said about the variables before. In each case the alternative hypothesis (H_a) refers to predictions derived from the theory. The null-hypothesis (H_0) forms its opposite, and states that no effect will be observable. In other words, H_0 states that the IV has no effect on the DV, while H_a claims that the IV has an effect on the DV. In the analysis of the data statistical techniques are employed to conclude which of the two hypotheses (H_0 or H_a) is to be accepted and which one is to be rejected. As is usual in test design, the formulation follows the principle that the null-hypothesis is a hypothesis of no differences and should therefore be the one that is to be rejected if the theory holds. It will be the case for some hypotheses, however, that it is the H_a that has to be rejected in favour of H_0. We shall return to this point below.

The first hypothesis concerns the variable of <u>memorability</u>. The question here is whether FG and BG can be observed as different categories in the responses of informants to a memory test. If the theory of FG holds, FG words that had been deleted would be recalled correctly with a statistically significant higher frequency than the items belonging to the BG of the text. H_0 on the other hand asserts that no such difference will be observable and that the number of correct recalls of both FG and BG items will depend only on chance. H_1 (from now on hypotheses will be numbered, to distinguish them from each other) however, states that such a difference <u>will</u> be apparent in the data, and that the direction of the difference is also predictable: FG items will be recalled correctly more often than BG items.

With regard to the postulate of <u>strikingness</u> it is assumed that words of the poem that are clearly FG will be underlined by the informants with a higher frequency than words that are BG, so that here again the direction of the outcome of the experiment is predicted. This then is H_2, specifying the prediction concerning the variable of strikingness as related to the theoretical construct of FG. H_0 in this case claims that no apparent difference in the frequency of underlining will be found in the data.

<u>Importance</u> is measured through the ranking of phrases from the text, presented as a randomized list of both FG and BG phrases. H_0 claims that these rankings (as carried out by subjects) will be random and will not display a significant correspondence to predictions based on a stylistic analysis of the FG in the text. H_3 alternatively postulates that informants' average rankings will correlate significantly with rankings predicted on the basis of the theoretical model and its application in text analysis as developed in Chapter 3.

The fourth of the initial postulates, <u>discussion value</u>, tested through an underlining test, may be cast in the form of the following hypothesis: informants will indicate FG configurations as possessing a higher discussion value than BG stretches of the text. Consequently H_4 predicts a high number of underlined words in parts of the text that are FG and a low frequency of underlinings in the BG passages. H_0 posits that any differences observed are the result of pure probability and that statistical analysis will therefore yield high p-values.

These then are the hypotheses concerning the four initial postulates. The fifth hypothesis relates to the constraints that operate in readers' confrontation with FG in a poem. More particularly it predicts that the influence of <u>individuality</u> will not be so powerful that it overrides the general consensus in reaction to the text. Hence, in this case the theoretical model predicts that H_0 will <u>not</u> be rejected. H_5 claims that individual differences between Ss' reactions will be so great that they are statistically significant. The theory of FG however will prefer H_0: reactions are not arbitrary and the consensus among subjects must be statistically significant.

In the case of the contribution FG makes to the <u>interpretation</u> of the text, it follows from the theory that H_0 has to be rejected. It claims that in Ss' indication of passages important for the interpretation of the poem, no difference will be found between passages that are FG and those that are BG. H_6 however predicts that such a difference will be apparent and that a significant positive effect will be observable in the direction of FG passages. In other words, FG configurations of the text will be indicated by Ss as contributing more to its interpretation than the BG parts of the poem.

<u>Repeated exposure</u> to the same poem was expected to have an effect of growing consensus among informants, even if they have had no opportunity to exchange ideas on the text. This is the prediction of H_7. Its corresponding H_0 asserts that no such effect will be apparent.

Concerning the <u>variety in the sample</u> H_8 affirms that generally the different hypotheses will be confirmed for different texts and with different groups of informants. Because we have specifically formulated hypotheses concerning the subgroups of informants, H_8 will be limited to the variety in <u>text</u> types, the prediction being that hypotheses will be confirmed by data for all text samples used as input material in the experiments. H_0 would predict that no such consistency may be found and that hypothesis confirmation will occur only on the basis of chance, i.e. with a fraction of the total text-sample only.

The three final hypotheses may be grouped together. In each case it is H_0 which is to be accepted according to the theory of FG. They predict that neither familiarity with the concept of FG (H_9), nor previously received literary training (H_{10}), nor the specific attitudes towards poetry, held by informants (H_{11}) will influence their responses to FG in the poems. If FG is functional in the reading of literature and if it is general in nature, as the theory claims, then none of these alternative hypotheses is to be accepted. Instead, for each of them H_0 (stating that no significant differences between subgroups composed on the basis of these three criteria will be found in the data) should be accepted. Analysis here will make use of cross-tabulation of the results obtained in the other experiments. From now on the various hypotheses will be referred to by the numbers they have been given above. For ease of reference, they are summarized, together with the proposed treatment of the data, in Table 2.2. (p. 51).

DESCRIPTION OF THE SAMPLE

This section concentrates on the sampling of informants; for a discussion of the sample of texts, see the following chapter. In this connection several points should be mentioned. It was decided at an early stage in the research programme to use university students as informants, because of their availability. Lindauer (1974: 178) also suggests students as a promising informant population. Against this decision, one could argue that such a sample is rather homogeneous and that therefore the experiments tell us little of how poetry is read in the world at large. Acknowledging that there is a danger in generalizing findings beyond the present horizon, attention should be drawn however to a serious methodological consideration: there is some evidence that the understanding of poetry is related to general intelligence; see Valentine (1962: 319). Moreover, Vergara's experiments, also discussed by Valentine (1962: 380-381) showed that, when IQ was low, oral presentation conveyed the meaning and mood of the poem better than silent reading. As it was intended to present the poems in the experiments through silent reading rather than through oral delivery for the sake of objectivity[6], this provides another reason to use students as informants. If these empirical studies hold, then according to the principle of moving from simple to more complex cases, it would seem wise to start the investigation with those informants who may be most likely to be good understanders of the texts being used. However, to counter the possibility of setting up a situation of self-fulfilling prediction, it was decided to include a fair number of informants in the sample who were (at least by university training) in no way acquainted with either the reading or the study of literature. The sample for the first series of experiments (apart from the pilot test) was therefore made up of three groups of second and third year students at the University of Lancaster, composed in the following way:

(1)   Students who had just finished a complete course in stylistics, and who had spent a fair amount of time on both stylistic theory in general and on the theory of foregrounding in particular. Although the matter was never mentioned explicitly and although they were instructed in exactly the same way as Ss belonging to other subgroups, it seems likely that a number of them may have grasped, albeit subconsciously, that the tests were geared towards certain aspects of the theory of foregrounding. (This subgroup will be named STY hereafter.)

(2)   A second subgroup consisted of undergraduates of the School of English, familiar with reading literature and with modes of literary analysis, but who had not done a stylistics course, and who almost certainly were not acquainted with the theory of FG. (This group was labelled the ENG-group.)

(3)   A third group consisted of informants who had no academic training whatsoever in the reading of literature. Most of them came from science departments, such as biology, chemistry, environmental sciences, physics, engineering, geography. A few also came from other humanities, such as sociology, history, politics, but care was taken not to include students of language departments, who might also have been acquainted with literature through their study of a foreign language. One may assume that the general knowledge of literary theory in this subgroup was far below that of the other two groups. (This subgroup, being composed of students not belonging to the School of English, was labelled the NENG-group.)

Thus a cline of expertise may be noticed in the composition of the sample: on the one hand there are the experimentally naive Ss (NENG-group). The ENG-group possesses some general knowledge of literary affairs, thereby occupying a middle ground, while the STY-group has experience of the FG model itself, and is therefore situated at the expert side of the cline.

PROCEDURES FOR DATA COLLECTION

Three different sessions were organized in order to test the hypotheses empirically. The first one was a pilot test, which will be discussed below. In the second session, all hypotheses outlined so far, except H_6 were tested. H_6 was tested in a third session, together with a number of assumptions concerning evaluative aspects of FG, to be reported in chapters 5 and 6 of this study. In each of these two sessions subjects were seated apart and were asked not to communicate with each other during the experiment. A pile of sheets which were turned face down had been arranged in front of them. As the experiment progressed Ss had to turn these over one by one. The sheets contained the test poems, instructions, tasks, and the Likert scales. All Ss were briefed in the same wording with regard to the aims of the experiments. The experimenter clarified these as investigating 'audience reactions to the reading of poetry', and that they would therefore be asked to read some short poems and then to comment on them. Oral instructions complemented the ones written on the sheets. These were read out to Ss by the experimenter. During the pilot test the times for reading the poems and for carrying out the tasks had been recorded, and averages of these were used in the experiment, so as not to let the factor of time influence the results. Participants were asked to work at a steady pace and to concentrate on the tasks. They were also told that the instructions were to be considered as complete. At one particular point in the first experiment a student wanted more information on what was meant by the word 'striking'. The experimenter answered that one was free to interpret the word in whatever sense one wished. In the second experiment a sentence to this effect was added to the oral instructions.

The order of the tests was as follows: first students were asked to fill in some personal details (their name, age, department, etc.) and then to fill in the Likert scales on poetry involvement. They then read the first poem at least twice, after which Part B, C, D and E were to be carried out. Then the second poem was read, with the same order of tests. Four such poems were read and commented on by the informants, thus bringing the total number of tasks carried out to 16. In order to counterbalance fatigue effects, a short break was held half-way through the experiments. Subjects could relax, stand up, have a walk in the corridor, or smoke, but were explicitly asked not to talk to each other during the break or afterwards. In the first experiment the order of presentation of the poems was the same for all participants, but in later tests this was not the case. It was thought that as concentration might diminish towards the end, such a fixed order might influence responses. For this reason the order of presentation of the texts was randomized throughout the group of informants. For specific instructions contained in the sheets or given orally, see Appendix 1.

TREATMENT OF THE DATA

The output from the experiments consists of data of different forms. In the case of the Likert scale these are positions on the scales; the underlining tests yield words that are underlined and words that are not underlined; the ranking tests provide allocated ranks, etc. All of these reactions of informants can be turned into quantitative data; the rankings can be used in their numerical form, and the number of times particular words have been underlined or recalled can be counted. Once such quantification has taken place, it also becomes possible to analyse the data with the help of statistical techniques. I should like to emphasize that in taking this course I thereby do not wish to adhere to any neo-positivist or reductionist doctrine. The major reason why quantification and statistical analysis was brought in lies in the fact that it allows for a greater degree of testability. By rigorously defining criteria for the analysis of the data beforehand, it becomes, because of the definiteness of such data, much easier to refute the theoretical model that is being investigated. Thus the use of quantitative methods adopted here is not, to quote Popper (1972: 356) an aim in itself, but only a means of putting theories to the test:

> This consideration also allows us to explain the demand that qualitative statements should if possible be replaced by quantitative ones by our principle of increasing the degree of testability of our theories. (In this way we can also explain the part played by measurement in the testing of theories; it is a device which becomes increasingly important in the course of scientific progress....)

Moreover, such quantitative techniques should complement intuitive scanning of the data and rational argumentation. Finally, any rational method examining data in this way would basically use the same method as the statistical techniques used, i.e. scan the data and estimate whether certain observed differences are large enough to lead to a specific conclusion. Statistical models merely perform the same kind of task, i.e. estimate differences, but in a more systematic and sophisticated way. Rational argumentation will be needed, however, to evaluate such quantitative methods and results.

The experiments carried out yield for the most part data collected in the <u>nominal</u> scale of measurement. This means that they consist of frequencies only. This is obvious in the memorability test: the number of times a deleted word has been recalled is what has been recorded. The underlining tests are quantified by counting the number of times each word had been underlined by the informants, thereby also yielding nominal frequencies. The Likert scale however, together with the ranking tests, yield data in the <u>ordinal</u> scale of measurement. This means that they not only indicate frequencies, but that they also contain information about the ordering of every individual observation with regard to its position relative to other observations. Thus ordinal data contain considerably more information than nominal data, and consequently allow a greater choice in techniques for statistical treatment. The nature of both kinds of data in most cases still asks for non-parametric statistics[7]. Another reason why these are to be preferred is that no strong assumptions about the underlying distribution in our results can be made yet.

Because in the present experiment the danger of committing a Type 1 error[8] is more likely than a Type 2 error, it was decided to put the level of significance[9] relatively low, i.e. at $p \leqslant .05$. The region of rejection (of every null-hypothesis) therefore consists of all values of statistics that are associated with p-values lower than .05.

Concerning errors, several measures were introduced in the design to counter any effects of constant errors. For instance, from the second session onwards, the order of the poems presented was randomized in order to counter a systematic fatigue effect. Although for some tests we have collected materials through questionnaires, in most cases this was done in experiments, where as many factors as possible were controlled, i.e. manner of instruction, presentation, timing, etc. This may not avoid all errors, but those left would be random rather than constant. With repeated experimentation the effects of random errors should cancel each other out.

The various statistical tools employed in the analysis were selected in advance. They have been grouped here according to the kind of data collected in the experiments. The nominal data are geared towards examining the existence of FG vs. BG as two discrete categories. Such a categorization of responses is imposed on administrative, not on theoretical grounds. Hence it is not assumed that FG and BG constitute two separate classes in a poetic text, but that in order to test the validity of the concepts themselves it may be advantageous, certainly at the beginning stage, to work with a simplified model in which they are treated as opposite poles. This entails that a certain amount of information (i.e. the arrangement along a continuum) is neglected in this aspect of the design. Hence these tests need to be complemented by experiments collecting data in the ordinal scale of measurement. For the nominal data then, the binomial test and the χ^2 -test of association are the appropriate non-parametric techniques available.

The ordinal data are more realistic and closer to the theoretical model in that they can be analysed without imposing some artificial categorization. Thus they test the theoretical predictions that FG and BG items in a poem are opposed in a relative way, and that consequently items in a poem may be arranged along a continuum, with FG and BG at both ends of the cline. As such the tests involved in this part of the design are stronger (i.e. riskier) tests than the ones employed with the nominal data. An appropriate statistic available for these tests is the Spearman Rank Correlation test.

Finally, there is one group of variables that has not been entered yet into the present discussion of test instruments, i.e. the hypotheses referring to the intersubjective consensus. These can be tested by the χ^2-test as goodness-of-fit test for the nominal data, and by the Kendall coefficient of concordance for the ordinal data. For the latter type of data, similar techniques are available, i.e. the Kruskal-Wallis one-way analysis of variance. The latter, together with the χ^2-test is an

appropriate technique used for testing differences between perform-
ances of subgroups, as is the Friedman two-way analysis of variance.

DESIGN OF STUDY AND PROCEDURE FOR ANALYSIS

In the previous sections of this chapter attention has been given
to the empirical variables derived from the general theory of FG, and
how these led to specific hypotheses. On the basis of these, a number
of experiments were designed and later carried out. In addition, the
type of data collected and the quantitative methods available for their
analysis have been outlined. It should be pointed out that such a prior
explication of analytical tools is of paramount importance to the
objective testing of theories. In order to make decisions about the
confirmation of a particular hypothesis it is imperative that an
objective procedure is laid down prior to the actual testing. Once this
has been clarified the collection of empirical data and their scoring can
begin. As a first step, it was decided to test a number of our materials
in a pilot session. This will be discussed next, as its results led to
further control of variables and facilitated the organization of later
experiments. Such discussion will profit from a summary of the main
points so far. For matters of clarity Table 2.2 lists the different
hypotheses that were developed, together with the particular test
situations in which they were verified and the analytical tools used to
examine the empirical data obtained in them.

Table 2.2 Summary of experimental design

Hypo-thesis	Postulate	Experi-ments	Data	Analysis procedure
H_1	Memorability	B	Nominal	Binomial; χ^2
H_2	Strikingness	C	Nominal	Binomial; χ^2
H_3	Importance	D	Ordinal	Spearman Rank Correlation
H_4	Discussion value	E	Nominal	Binomial; χ^2
H_5	Individuality	B,C,E,F D,F	Nominal Ordinal	χ^2 goodness-of-fit Kendall's W
H_6	Cohesion/ Contribution to Interpretation	F	Nominal	Binomial; χ^2 goodness-of-fit
			Ordinal	Spearman Rank Correlation
H_7	Repeated Exposure	C/E	Nominal	Non-quantitative; χ^2 goodness-of-fit
H_8	Sample variety	A-F	Nominal Ordinal	Non-quantitative
H_9	Familiarity with the theory	B-E	Nominal Ordinal	χ^2 Kruskal-Wallis; Friedman
H_{10}	Literary training	B-E	Nominal Ordinal	χ^2 Kruskal-Wallis; Friedman
H_{11}	Attitudes to poetry	A	Nominal Ordinal	Binomial; χ^2 Spearman Rank Correlation

THE PILOT TEST

A pilot experiment was conducted in two different sessions, each time in as much the same conditions as was possible. The sample of informants consisted of 9 undergraduate students, with 3 students in each of the subgroups. Two poems were used as test material, the one by Cummings and the one by Roethke (see Chapter 3). Informants were asked to fill in the Likert scales, and then to read the first poem. The tasks they had to carry out were identical for the two poems. In the first one they had to write down (after they had turned over the sheet with the poem) all they could remember of the poem on a separate sheet. Next they were presented with a version of the poem in which a number of words had been deleted. The following test consisted in underlining those passages they found 'clearest for what the poet was trying to do'. In the fourth and final part they were presented with a number of words from the poem that had been grouped into triads. Ss were then asked to indicate which word in each triad they judged as most important.

During each of these tasks the experimenter recorded the time needed by every subject. The average time for the nine Ss was calculated and used as guidance in the later experiments. After the experiment, Ss were asked to write down any comments they had on the actual tasks. Inspection of these comments revealed that the major difficulties encountered by most of the participants occurred in the memory test and in the final task in which the most important word had to be selected from a group of three. Several subjects reported that they found it extremely difficult to attach importance to single words, isolated from their context. They did not find the test tiring or boring, but more than half of them found the tasks very hard to carry out. Finally, during the first session there was some confusion among Ss concerning the instructions of the underlining task. Consequently the wording of the oral instructions for this part was altered. No such confusion arose in the second session or in later experiments which used these instructions.

When the results themselves were investigated, some important findings emerged. First of all, both memory tests seemed to have their own particular problems. The free recall test provided lots of data, but a serious difficulty was found in the fact that the picture from this test was extremely diffuse. Ss seemed to remember different things and little correspondence could be detected between the protocols of different subjects. Moreover it was often quite difficult to decipher some of the responses, sometimes due to careless writing, but more often because the item recalled was not in the original text, without it being clear from the response which one it supposedly referred to. Finally, it proved almost impossible to quantify these data in any objective way. The other memory test consisted in filling out blanks in the text, where words had been deleted. Here doubt over the correctness of a recall was non-existent; there was no difficulty in quantifying the responses, and the experimenter had complete control over the dependent variable. (He could, for instance, delete an equal number of both FG and BG words, something which was not possible in the free recall test.) But considerably less data were generated by this test, and as some of the poems (e.g. the one by Cummings) were rather short, it was difficult to imagine a version of the text from which a lot of words had been removed. Moreover, both memory tests yielded data that made one suspicious of the hypothesis. In some cases it was quite obvious that items from the BG were recalled with greater frequency than the FG items. It seemed therefore that the opposite of what had been predicted had happened: FG seemed to be more difficult to remember. Could it be that a given deviation was obliterated in memory because of its idiosyncratic characteristics? On the basis of these observations it was decided to use only one test of recall in later experiments. The cloze-version of the memory test was preferred, because of its superior qualities in terms of control over variables by the experimenter and because of the unambiguity in scoring and quantifying the data.

The underlining test seemed to answer best to our needs, and hence this test was retained in the final form of the experiments, but

53

as stated before, its wording was improved. It was also used later as a test for the hypothesis concerning the discussion value of FG items.

Finally, with the test that asked Ss to select the most important word from a group of three, the picture was quite diffuse. Since several Ss had pointed in their comments to the extreme difficulty in carrying out this task, it was decided to eliminate it from future experiments. It was replaced by Part D, which consisted of presenting Ss with a randomized list of phrases from the poem they were asked to rank in their order of importance. Later, in Part F, Ss were simply asked to rank order verse-lines.

One final point should be mentioned here. Each of the poems used was accompanied with a question whether Ss had ever read the particular poem before, or whether they recognized its author. Although few participants gave positive replies, it was nevertheless found significant that some of them actually succeeded in identifying the text or the author. For this reason it was thought an interesting question to retain in later experiments. If, for instance, too many Ss knew the poem, then this might influence their reactions in the experiments. Such factors might then exert an influence without being known to the experimenter.

CONCLUSION

This chapter has concentrated on the way in which the experiments set up to test the theory were developed. As none of the people involved with this study had at that time any serious grasp of methods in social psychology, such an enterprise proved to be quite challenging, especially as no similar research preceded it in the field of stylistics. For this reason it should not be left unmentioned that, although from the very beginning the effort had been to work consistently towards usable tools and testable hypotheses, these were only arrived at gradually and in the course of time. What has emerged is a design that, although perhaps not being wholly failsafe in all respects, should certainly yield results highlighting the relationship between textual structure and reader response. We will return to the tests later, but at this point we will move on to examine in detail the way the concrete predictions used in the experiments were arrived at. This will be done in Chapter 3. After the presentation of these stylistic analyses, Chapter 4 will resume the empirical thread and examine the results of the experiments.

NOTES

1. For a more detailed account of the 'Von Restorff effect', see Keele (1973: 36-38).

2. The term is used in its technical sense, referring to aspects of the independent variable, i.e. the (two) values the IV can take. For a clarification of these (and similar) concepts, see Anastasi (1966), Oppenheim (1966), Robson (1973) and Siegel (1956).

3. See, for a summary of these views, Lindauer (1974: 29-35, 170, 183).

4. Such a procedure was also followed for some other test instruments: some alternatives were thought out and then put to the test in the pilot session.

5. See Oppenheim (1966: 133-142).

6. One might argue that an oral delivery cannot avoid imposing some kind of interpretation on the text. A presentation of the poem in as neutral a form as possible was needed in order not to bias informants in any particular direction.

7. See Robson (1973: 106-114) and Siegel (1956: expecially 30-34).

8. This error is made when it is thought that the IV had an effect on the DV, when in fact it had not. A Type 2 error is the reverse of this, i.e. when one fails to see that the IV had an effect on the DV. See, for instance, Robson (1973: 34-35).

9. This measure indicates the probability level below which one is prepared to reject H_0, and to accept that the IV had an effect on the DV.

Chapter Three

ANALYSES OF THE POEMS AND PREDICTIONS MADE

INTRODUCTION

This chapter will look in some detail at the texts that were used as test material in the experiments. There can be little doubt as to the importance of the actual analyses of the poems carried out. Any testing of the theory of foregrounding depends for its validity on the objectivity with which the predictions based on the theory are arrived at. Evidence in favour of, or against, the theoretical model may be illusory if the analyses of the texts used in testing are unreliable. Yet in this respect, stylistic theory and practice are still highly vulnerable. This vulnerability lies in the fact that stylistics does not provide a failsafe algorithm for the analysis of texts. Or, in the words of Fowler (1984: 173):

there is a common misconception that linguistics - any linguistics - is a kind of automatic analyzing device which, fed a text, will output a description without human intervention.

In terms of the analyses of poems that were needed for experimentation of the kind outlined in the previous chapter, this would entail that different analysts would come up with different results of their analyses. How to solve the indispensibility of an objective analysis was the major problem which had to be addressed. The solution developed and reported in this chapter has been, out of necessity, a pragmatic one. Under the present circumstances, all one can hope for in such matters is a descriptive procedure which is <u>as objective as possible</u>, and which allows for a maximum of intersubjective control, rather than any objectivity in an 'absolute' sense. The analyses presented here should be viewed in this light. Every effort has been taken to minimize the influence of the analyst's own presuppositions with regard to the text, and wherever feasible, criteria for description have been made as explicit as possible. The result is, I believe, a descriptive analysis which, although not being objective in an absolute sense, is nevertheless objective, first of all in the sense that the procedures leading to it are controllable, secondly in the sense that the outcome of the analyses are only to be disputed marginally. By and large, this holds more for the levels of phonological and grammatical analyses than for the semantic level; compare also Fowler (1984: 183).

As a final preliminary, a limitation of this chapter should be pointed out in advance. Owing to space restrictions a fully-fledged analysis (in the sense of being as exhaustive as necessary) of each of the poems is not possible. Such an enterprise would constitute nearly a whole volume in its own right. Consequently, only the major aspects of the analyses undertaken can be dealt with. What is presented here, however, is a summary of highly detailed and lengthy analyses, reported in Van Peer (1980), in which every care had been taken to employ categories as objective as possible for the detection and classification of devices displayed by the texts. In what follows, the general principles for the selection of texts and the methods used in analysing them, as well as the scoring system developed, will be commented on, followed by a characterization of each of the poems, accompanied by the major dimensions of FG as identified in the analyses. The outline of each poem will then conclude with the predictions made, as based on a visual representation of FG locations in the text.

COMPOSITION OF THE TEXT-CORPUS

Since the aim was to make generalizations about readers' responses to any given text, it was imperative to avoid any bias in the composition of the text-corpus and to make it as representative as possible. On the other hand it was practically difficult to work with a large corpus because of the large amount of time involved in preparing full-scale stylistic analyses of even short texts. This dual demand of representativeness and workability from an administrative point of view put some constraints on the selection of texts that could be made. It ruled out the possibility, for instance, of working with novels or drama. In other words, where diversity and conciseness were simultaneously needed, the process of text-selection had to be carried out with care. This led, at an early stage in the design of the study, to the decision to use poetry texts in the experiments. This generic restriction imposed on the text-corpus made it possible to work with relatively short texts, while their literary character could hardly be doubted. In order to safeguard this character still further, it was also decided to use poems by major poets in the English language, whose literary qualities could hardly be questioned. In order to control factors such as time and fatigue in the experimental situation it was furthermore decided to use texts of 'average' length within the domain of lyrical poems, i.e. poems which could be read within a few minutes.

The selectional procedure gains force from general methodological considerations too, as outlined by Lindauer (1974: 181), who suggests that empirical research on literature should strike a balance between a reductionist approach and the broad requirements of literary relevance. To this end it is profitable to work with short literary forms, such as poetry and quotations. These serve the purposes of reductions, but at the same time, unlike nonsense material, they preserve their basic aesthetic and literary qualities. They also make the research manageable from a procedural and quantificational point of view.

The decision to choose poetry as test material may also be defended from yet another angle. It cannot be denied that most of the theoretical work on FG has taken poetic texts as its primary source for illustration and analysis. This does not entail that the presence of FG in longer literary works, or in prose, is denied or doubted. Indeed it would be surprising if the same processes would not work in a very similar way in longer literary works of art: see, for instance, the studies of Groos (1975) and of Moser (1974). But - apart from some exceptional works - it is likely that FG in such longer works might appear in a more diluted form. Hence its effects on a reader might be more difficult to observe. In this respect, an explorative study into the psychological validity of FG has to obey the maxim of progressing from the simple to the more complex. Therefore it is advantageous to use types of texts in which FG could be observed in its most condensed way, and in which it could be pointed at most easily. There can be little doubt that, at least as far as recent Western literature goes, lyrical poetry meets this demand more than any other genre. Thus the decision to take poetic texts as the starting-point for the design of experiments was not a purely administrative one, but involved theoretical reflections on the nature of FG and its operation in the reading process as well as general considerations of empirical design.

A further delimitation concerns the form and content of the poems. Since all individuals should have equal chances to express their reaction to FG it was decided to exclude any poems which for their interpretation were strongly dependent on historical, cultural, literary or linguistic knowledge, on mythological references, or the like. Hence poems requiring more than elementary knowledge of cultural context were judged ill-suited to the purpose under consideration. This led to the exclusion of poems older than the 19th century, on the ground that the language and the cultural conventions of earlier periods would present supplementary difficulties to informants without literary training. The variable of being acquainted with older modes of literature would then take over and bias results in favour of the trained subjects.

A related restriction bears on the fact that the study was first and foremost aimed at the exploration of the effects of FG as caused by the language of texts. This is not to deny that other factors, such as literary conventions or traditional cultural expectations, might not play a role too. However, as the present study was conceived of from a linguistic viewpoint, it was thought wise to exclude factors which would go far beyond the confines of such a framework, and which, for the sake of hypothesis testing, might impede a sharp focus in design and analysis. More important still, since the crucial point was to find out whether (linguistically caused) effects of FG could be observed in the responses of readers, the corpus had to be balanced in such a way that it offered all Ss equal chances of demonstrating the effects of FG in the text. In this sense our readers are to be considered as the opposite of Fish's informed reader; see Fish (1970). They should be naive with respect to traditional knowledge about particular (types of) literary texts. It was therefore decided to work with poems that, although written by well-known authors, would be virtually unknown to the informants. Such a decision also gains strength from the following perspective: if the poems presented were known to readers, factors of author-prestige could influence responses. It has been shown that aesthetic preference can be modified experimentally. More specifically, Chapman & Williams (1976) and Eisenmann & Boss (1970) demonstrated that when rating was done after exposure to favourable information on the artist to which the work was ascribed, ratings changed to a greater degree of liking. Since some of the present experiments involved subjective measures of preference, it was important to mask the origin of all texts employed. Only in this way is it possible to arrive at subjects' preferences and to eliminate effects due to prestige of author or period.

Within the confines outlined previously, a more or less intuitive choice of poems was made, with one guiding principle in mind: to provide as wide a variety of texts as possible. A close look at the six poems finally selected reveals the different backgrounds: three poems were written in the 19th and three in the 20th century. Two are by American poets (Dickinson, Cummings), and four by British poets. They can easily be arranged along a scale of increasing modernism, with

Rossetti and Wordsworth at one end of the scale, going via Dickinson and Roethke in the middle to Thomas and Cummings as the ones showing the highest degree of modernism. Although they are all lyrical poems of 'standard' format, there is also some variation in their length: compare the poem by Cummings (approximately 40 words) with the one by Roethke (approximately 100 words). A rough indication of the content of the poems shows the themes to vary considerably too: love (Cummings), man's intellect vs. the world and infinity (Dickinson), human emotion vs. bureaucracy (Roethke), lost hope and dreams (Rossetti), lost childhood (Thomas), nature (Wordsworth).

GENERAL METHOD OF TEXT ANALYSIS

Apart from selectional procedures as described in the previous section, serious considerations had to be given to the nature of the analyses leading to the concrete predictions that had to be used in the experiments. The aim was to describe the linguistic material of the texts in such a way that from the description itself it was possible to derive predictions as to the location of FG in the poem. Of course one could go about it in a more intuitive way, by pinpointing FG on the basis of one's own linguistic competence, literary experience or cultural knowledge. Profitable though such an approach may be, it was found wanting for the purposes of the present study. Methodological considerations require an intensive scanning of the poem, and to carry this out according to a controllable procedure. Only by following such a procedure will it be possible for other researchers in the field to verify the analyses. Insofar as the theory of FG allows for the making of predictions, the decision-making process has to be objectified. To make the link between such predictions and observable cases of FG in the text more explicit, an intensive analysis of each poem is indispensable. Note that by 'intensive' is not meant an exhaustive, or final analysis, (such an aim could be claimed to be theoretically impossible), but simply to indicate that a detailed, systematic, and explicit investigation of virtually all stylistic phenomena on different levels of linguistic organization had been carried out.

The position taken in the previous paragraph entails that a rough quantification of FG has to be the end-product of the analyses. Indeed, in the absence of any insight into the proportional contribution of the various FG devices as identified by the analyses, hardly any predictions could be made. As a starting-point for such a quantification, the elements mentioned in the 'standard' version of the theory of FG (see the end of Chapter 1) could be used. First of all, the different devices whereby FG is produced, may be distinguised from each other. Parallelism and the three different types of deviation (internal, determinate, statistical) are taken as separate configurations which may be located within the text of the poem. Their identification, although not completely mechanical, could nevertheless be undertaken with some reliability, in the sense that different analysts might largely agree on what is deviant (and in what sense), and what should be considered as parallel. Yet such a categorization was still found an insufficient guarantee against possible subjectivity in scoring. Therefore, the identification of the different types of FG was carried out in three successive stages, corresponding to three conventional levels of linguistic description: phonology, grammar, and semantics. Each descriptive level was treated in its own right, and the activities concerning each of the levels were carried out separately. (For a rationale of this method, see Crystal & Davy (1969), especially Chapter Two.) It was furthermore assumed that higher levels of language, such as the semantic organization of the text, will contribute more to the overall effect than the respective lower levels, such as grammar or phonology, although the effects of different layers may partly overlap. Whether this assumption would lead to accurate predictions, would then have to be confirmed by the empirical results.

The analysis of each of the descriptive levels was carried out in the following way. For the phonological level, a phonetic transcription of each of the poems was prepared on the basis of Gimson (1962). These transcriptions tried to capture as neutral as possible a reading of the text. It will be appreciated that this was not always an easy matter. For instance, when to transcribe a vowel as / / in RP was not always straightforward. In general, the transcriptions tried to strike a balance between a highly abstract phonological transcription and a phonetic rendering of an RP delivery. Although differences of opinion may arise over certain small-scale decisions, such cases should only rarely have major implications for the conclusions drawn from the analyses.

On the basis of the transcriptions an accurate investigation of all forms of parallelism and deviation was made. For parallelism, this presented little difficulty, as traditional poetics has occupied itself extensively with this type of device on the phonological level. Furthermore, it may be predicted that by and large determinate deviation on this level will be rare. Internal deviation had - as was the case for the levels of grammar and semantics too - to be analysed on the basis of a detailed scanning of each of the poems separately. Concerning the statistical deviations on this level, it is possible to make comparative statements on phoneme frequencies. For this purpose, I have relied on Fry's counts of average frequency in British English. Although this research is now rather old, I have nevertheless preferred it to Roberts, A.H.: A Statistical Linguistic Analysis of American English (Mouton 1965). Although this work is more recent and no doubt based on much more thorough research, this work is completely oriented toward American English, and may therefore be less well adapted to our purposes. Moreover, the fact that Fry's tables are still quoted in the 1978 edition of Gimson (1962: 148, 219) provides an indication of its representativeness.

For the level of grammar, a detailed analysis of morphological and syntactic structures of the texts was made. Use was made of both structural and generative insights into grammatical structure. For instance, Chomsky (1964) was used as a guideline for categorization of diverse forms of determinate deviation. Statistical and internal deviation were identified on the basis of a minute exploration of the various syntactic configurations of the text. As to the detection of parallelism, this was founded on the recurrent features that could be observed in the structures revealed by the grammatical analysis. In general, a frequent problem encountered was whether to categorize particular instances of FG devices as manifestations on either the grammatical or semantic level. For instance, violations of selection restrictions or of subcategorization rules could be dealt with under both headings. Since the level of semantics played a more important role in the scoring system used (see further), the FG devices concerned were upgraded, i.e. categorized as semantic phenomena, wherever this was possible. In this way FG structures identified in the text were, so to say, given the benefit of the doubt, and were treated in the 'highest' level of description, so as not to underscore their importance in the making of predictions.

In general, considerations about lexis are also discussed under the heading of semantics. Although there may be reasons to categorize these under the level of grammar too, as they are also concerned with the formal aspects of language, it was judged necessary to study them under the heading of semantics, mainly because of the special instances in which they would be encountered in the poetic texts. Wherever lexical deviation or parallelism operates in the texts, it can hardly be doubted that it will have a strong impact on the meaning of that part of the text, or on the meaning of the text as a whole. Moreover, rather than introducing a separate level for the analysis of lexis, a more economic solution was preferred, by including lexis in one of the levels already established, but to make the decisions concerned as explicit as possible. In some cases, as in the poem by E.E. Cummings and in the one by Roethke, some such FG structures have been treated under the heading of grammar, because this was more in line with the general structure of the text, or with Thorne's (1970) treatment of the poem.

Concerning the level of semantics properly speaking, it was - as has been pointed out already - the level at which most difficulties in description and categorization were encountered. Statistical deviation generally is rare on this level, and internal deviation could only be located with respect to the description of the rest of the text. Determinate deviation, which occurred most frequently of all types of deviation, was generally not too hard to detect, either with reference to grammatical rules, or with respect to lexicological definitions or descriptions based on world knowledge. Issues of semantic parallelism, occurring also relatively frequently, were identified on the basis of patterns of equivalence and/or contrast between meaning aspects of the items concerned. These may be based on the results of componential analysis, identity of propositional structure, negation of earlier propositions, contrasts between predicates, and the like. Thus, although often it was not possible for the description on the semantic level to be as objective as on the level of phonology or grammar, much care has been taken to make these descriptions as valid and reliable as possible.

Finally, for all levels of descriptions, extensive use was made of the descriptive tools offered by present-day linguistics, but - as may already have been apparent - in an eclectic way, assuming that different linguistic models serve different aims, and may therefore bring different advantages to the analysis of texts. Simultaneously, but this will be evident to the reader, the existing literature on stylistics was brought to bear on the issues concerning the analysis and description of the poems. In this way it was hoped to arrive at analyses of the texts which, although perhaps not being identical to the results of analyses that would be carried out by other stylisticians, would nevertheless present a level of objectivity that would raise the making of predictions above the merely subjective level of personal projections or of inflated idiosyncratic presuppositions vis-à-vis the text.

The combination of types of FG devices with different descriptive levels leads to a categorization of twelve different classes of FG: four devices, each of them potentially situated on three different levels of linguistic organization. To distinguish these different kinds of FG, a scoring system was developed in order to indicate text passages in which they could be identified. This greatly facilitated the recognition of the different kinds of FG in the text, and allowed for a visual representation of FG within a text. This was done in the following way. A widely spaced typed-out version of the poem was prepared, and used

Analyses of the poems and predictions made

as a visual 'display' of the text. After the stylistic analyses had been carried out, the different kinds of FG devices on the three linguistic levels were indicated with the help of the following symbols:

LEVELS OF LINGUISTIC DESCRIPTION	TYPES OF FG DEVICES
............: Phonology	☐ : parallelism
	0 : internal deviation
_____ : Grammar	X : determinate deviation
[_____]: Semantics	△ : statistical deviation

The geometric figures used to indicate types of FG devices were drawn at the beginning of the lines or frames indicating the different levels of description. For instance, the phonological parallelism of alliteration in Coleridge's

the furrow followed free

would be marked in the following way:

the furrow followed free
☐ ᴖᴖᴖ   ☐ ᴖᴖᴖ   ☐ ᴖᴖᴖ

A determinate deviation on the grammatical level, such as Hopkins'

let Him easter in us

would be marked:

let Him easter in us
X ————

As may be noted, the geometric figures indicating FG devices represent the same 'weight', but this is not the case for the symbols used to indicate the levels of description. In a visual graph containing all symbols for all kinds of FG, the dotted lines (for the phonological level) will be less conspicuous than the full lines representing the grammatical level, and these in turn will be less prominent than the frames holding the devices situated on the semantic level. This was done deliberately, in order to meet the requirement entailed in the assumption that 'higher' levels of organization, such as semantics, will presumably work more powerfully than the lower levels. It may be useful here to refer to Chapter 6, where this assumption will be put to the test. For the time being, however, this intuitive assumption (based, of course, on a view of reading, i.e. that people generally will tend to look for meaning in reading first, and will give secondary attention to formal or phonological structures) was operationalized through the difference in visual perspicuity the symbols carry.

A related point concerns the concepts of cohesion and of density, as outlined in the 'standard' version of the theory of FG at the end of Chapter 1. The former presents few problems for the system of representation that was adopted: different locations of the same, or similar FG devices in the linear structure of the text were identified and graphically indicated at these different locations. The situation is not very different for the concept of density. The devices identified on the three levels will, when superimposed on each other, reveal textual configurations where a nexus of FG may be identified. As such the visual representations prepared in the course of the descriptive analyses simultaneously reveal cohesion and density of FG in the text. It is obvious that text locations with a high density of FG should be given greater weight in the final quantification of FG. It was mainly on the basis of such superimposed density that decisions concerning an item belonging to either FG or BG had to be taken.

This leaves a final problem to be solved. In order to somehow work towards concrete predictions after the analysis and its visual representation, some kind of unit for 'passages' in the poem that would be FG or BG (or in between) was needed. Stated otherwise, in order to compare the density of FG in different passages of the poem, it was necessary to clarify what was meant by 'passage'. As no readily convenient method presented itself, it was decided to use verse-lines as units in this respect, as this is a traditional and conventional unit that is fairly well established in poetry composition and reception. Because there is no reason to suppose that FG is apprehended by readers in a line-by-line fashion, the use of lines as standard units is unfavourable to the theory of FG and its hypotheses. Its choice therefore does not undermine the validity of the test results. Hence verse-lines were allocated to the categories FG, BG, and in most poems also MG ('middle ground': those lines in between the FG and BG positions) on the basis of the graphs depicting the superimposed types and levels of FG devices. The poem by Wordsworth, containing only eight lines, was judged too short to be provided with a MG-category.

DESCRIPTIVE ANALYSES OF THE TEXTS

In what follows, each of the six poems used in the experiments will receive attention. The text of the poem will be presented first, together with a short abstract of the theme and the major dimensions of FG followed by an enumeration of FG devices on the three levels of description, each level containing the inventory of the four types of FG devices. The visual representation of the poem, with the symbols corresponding to the listed devices on the different descriptive levels, will then follow. Finally, both a division of verse-lines into the FG/(MG)/BG categories, as well as ranks allocated to verse-lines on the basis of the visual representation, will be provided. It is on the basis of these categorizations and ranks (which will be used as predictions) that the hypotheses concerning FG will be put to the test.

Analyses of the poems and predictions made

'yes is a pleasant country' by E.E. Cummings[1]

1	yes is a pleasant country:
2	if's wintry
3	(my lovely)
4	let's open the year
5	both is the very weather
6	(not either)
7	my treasure,
8	when violets appear
9	love is a deeper season
10	than reason;
11	my sweet one
12	(and april's where we're)

The poem by E.E. Cummings was selected because his poetry is often referred to as an illustrative example of how deviance of different kinds can manifest itself in poetry. It is extremely short: only forty words, with heavy deviance of semantic restrictions, lexical and syntactical rules, and even of a phonological norm. It has a traditional stanzaic outlook, which contradicts the strong violations apparent in the text. It is on a traditional theme of spring and love, in which a high amount of parallelism and cohesion binds together all elements tightly. The whole presents itself at first glance as a simple traditional poem, but on close inspection turns out to be one of extreme strangeness.

I. Inventory of FG devices:

PHONOLOGY
Statistical Deviation:
- brackets in the final verse-line
- consonant clusters in lines 1, 2, 7, 9, 10, 11, 12
- the vowels / / and /e/ in lines 1-2, 5-7
- diphthongs in lines 4, 8, and 12
- /l/ phoneme in lines 3-4

- /w/ phoneme in lines 11-12
- / / phoneme in lines 5-6
- plosives in line 1
- fricatives in lines 5 and 9
- the /i:/ vowel in lines 9-11

Determinate Deviation:
- additional stress on closed system items in lines 1, 2, 5
- colon in line 11
- 'april' without capital letter
- stress on 're' in line 12

Internal Deviation:
- stress on 'if' in line 2
- no contracted verb-form in line 8
- no tone-boundary at end of line 9
- first full rhyme in lines 9-10
- strong enjambement between 9-10
- 'love' in line 9 in similar stress position as 'yes' and 'both' in lines 1 and 5, but not belonging to a closed set

Parallelism:
- contrast: 'is' vs. contracted forms in lines 2, 4, 9, 12
- / / rhymes in lines 4, 8, 12
- half-rhymes in lines 1/3, 5/7
- rhymes in lines 9-10
- chiming of vowels in lines 1, 2, 4/5, 6/8, 5/8, 9/11

II. GRAMMAR

Statistical Deviation:
line 5: 'the very weather'

Determinate Deviation:
- Lexical rule violations in lines 1, 2, 5, 6
- Selection restriction violations in lines 1, 2, 4, 5, 9, 10, 12

Internal Deviation:
- growing complexity in lines 8-12 (except 11)
- only plural in line 8
- only cleft sentence in line 12
- 'love' in line 9 is not a lexical rule violation as in lines 1, 5
- only negative in line 6
- lines 9-10 contain the only case where syntactic and typographic patterns do not coincide (enjambement)

Parallelism:
Notice that the observed parallelisms in the syntax pose a problem here, because so many verse-lines are parallel, in the following way:
- lines 1, 5, 9
- lines 3, 7, 11

It is not so clear in what way one might distinguish the importance of these different cases of parallelism. This is a difficulty we shall also meet in the other poems.

III. SEMANTICS

Statistical Deviation:
- low number of linking words
- tendency towards dialogue, informal and familiar register

Determinate Deviation:
- (deep structure rule violations described in the section on grammar)
- new, symbolic meanings for the words: 'yes', 'country', 'if', 'wintry', 'both', 'weather', 'either', 'season', 'april', 'deeper'

Internal Deviation:
- 'violets' in line 8 is the only concrete noun
- 'wintry' in line 2 is the only predicative modifier
- 'love' in line 9 is first explicit statement of theme
- only wh-adjective in lines 8 and 12
- 'we' in line 12 unexpected after previous 'my'
- 'when' and 'and' in lines 8, 12: only linkers

Parallelism:
- equivalence relations:

yes	= pleasant country	(line 1)
if	= wintry	(line 2)
both	= very weather	(line 5)
love	=deeper season	(line 9)
april	= where	(line 12)

- contrasts: pleasant/wintry; love/reason; both/either; yes/if
- similarities in meaning:
  'open' (line 4)/ 'appear' (line 8)/ 'april' (line 12)

FIG. 3.1 VISUAL REPRESENTATION OF FG IN CUMMINGS' POEM

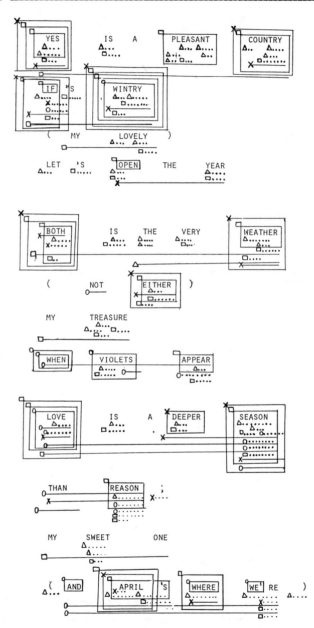

TABLE 3.1 PREDICTIONS: CUMMINGS

Ranks given to lines

Line	Rank
1	2
2	3
3	11
4	8
5	5
6	6
7	12
8	7
9	1
10	9
11	10
12	4

Division of lines
FG: 1, 2, 5, 9, 12
MG: 4, 6, 8, 10
BG: 3, 7, 11

'The Brain is wider than the Sky', by Emily Dickinson[2]

1   The Brain - is wider than the Sky -

2   For - put them side by side -

3   The one the other will contain

4   With ease - and You - beside -

5   The Brain is deeper than the sea -

6   For - hold them - Blue to Blue -

7   The one the other will absorb -

8   As Sponges - Buckets - do

9   The Brain is just the weight of God -

10   For - Heft them - Pound for Pound -

11   And they will differ - if they do -

12   As Syllable from Sound -

This less well-known poem on the theme of man and infinity by Emily Dickinson was selected as the second stimulus text. It takes the form of a string of analogies: the (human) brain is compared successively to the sky, the sea, and to God, in traditional stanzas that rhyme. The poem is highly metaphorical, the deviational aspects of its FG depending on knowledge of the world. At the same time it shows a high degree of parallelism.

Inventory of FG devices

I. PHONOLOGY

Statistical Deviation:
- /ɪ/ in lines 8, 11
- /ʌ/ in lines 7-8
- /uː/ in line 6
- /aɪ/ in lines 1-2
- /eɪ/ in lines 9, 11
- /iː/ in line 5
- /aʊ/ in line 10
- /l/ in line 6
- /b/ in lines 6-7
- /f/ and /p/ in line 10

Determinate Deviation:
- capital letters in 'Brain' (lines 1, 5, 9) 'Sky', 'Sponges', 'Buckets', 'Pound', 'Syllable', 'Sound'
- dash in line 1, 8

Internal Deviation:
- capital letters in 'You', 'Blue', 'Heft' (not nouns)
- lines 8, 12: (less monosyllabic words than in other lines)
- /g/ in line 9: only instance of this phoneme
- /j/ in line 4: only instance of this phoneme
- /dʒ/ in lines 8-9: only instance of this phoneme
- 'syllable' in line 12: stress pattern vs. metre
- defeated metrical expectancy in lines 9, 11, 12

Parallelism:
- rhymes: side-beside; blue-do (8, 11) and You (4); pound-sound; brain-contain (1, 3, 5)
- assonance:

line 1:	wider-sky
line 2:	side by side
lines 3, 4:	will, with, beside
line 5:	deeper, sea, ease
lines 3, 7:	one, other
line 8:	Sponges, Buckets, just
line 9:	Brain, weight
lines 11, 12:	will, differ, if, Syllable

- alliterations:

lines 1, 5:	than, the
lines 3, 7:	the, the, other
lines 3, 7:	one, will, (with)

line 11:	differ, do
line 12:	syllable, sound

II. GRAMMAR
Statistical Deviation:
inversion in line 8
Determinate Deviation:
none
Internal Deviation:
- line 9 (from pattern in lines 1, 5)
- line 11 (from pattern in lines 3, 7)
- plural nouns in line 8
- plural verbs in lines 8, 11 (the only such cases)
- future tense in line 11
Parallelism:
- lines 1, 5
- lines 2, 6, 10
- lines 3, 7
- lines 8, 12
- lines 11, 12

(Note again how little discrimination in text locations of FG can be made in this way: nearly all lines in the poem are parallel with some other line.)

III. SEMANTICS
Statistical Deviation:
- 'heft' (line 10)
- 'blue to blue' (line 6)
- 'God' (line 9), and 'syllable' (line 12): unexpected
Determinate Deviation:
- Selection restriction violations in lines 1, 5, 9
- violations of rules of logic in stanza 3
- figurative meanings apparent in key-words
Internal Deviation:
- abstract nouns in stanza 3 and 'ease' in line 4
- line 9 (not possible to disambiguate by assigning figurative meaning as in lines 1, 5)
- 'differ' in line 11: different from verbs in parallel lines
- 'the' in line 9: only cataphoric reference
- 'God' deviates from pattern: sea, sky
- line 9: equality instead of difference, as in preceding stanzas
Parallelism:
- patterned selection restriction violations in lines 1, 5, and 9
- sea, sky; wider, deeper; put, hold, heft

FIG. 3.2 VISUAL REPRESENTATION OF FG IN DICKINSON'S POEM

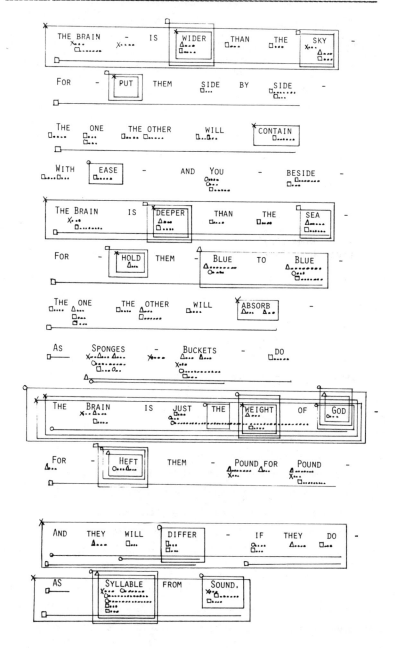

TABLE 3.2 PREDICTIONS: DICKINSON

Ranks given to lines

Line	Rank
1	2
2	11
3	10
4	8
5	4
6	9
7	12
8	6
9	1
10	7
11	5
12	3

Division of lines
FG: 1, 5, 9, 12
MG: 4, 8, 10, 11
BG: 2, 3, 6, 7

'Dolour' by Theodore Roethke[3]

1   I have known the inexorable sadness of pencils,

2   Neat in their boxes, dolour of pad and paperweight,

3   All the misery of manila folders and mucilage,

4   Desolation in immaculate public places,

5   Lonely reception room, lavatory, switchboard,

6   The unalterable pathos of basin and pitcher,

7   Ritual of multigraph, paper-clip, comma,

8   Endless duplication of lives and objects.

9   And I have seen dust from the walls of institutions,

10   Finer than flour, alive, more dangerous than silica,

11   Sift, almost invisible, through long afternoons of tedium,

12   Dropping a fine film on nails and delicate eyebrows,

13   Glazing the pale hair, the duplicate grey standard faces.

This poem by Theodore Roethke is discussed by Thorne (1970). The basic opposition + HUMAN versus - HUMAN pervades the whole text, bringing home the idea of emptiness and sterility as a result of the bureaucratization of man. Human emotions (sadness, pathos, dolour, etc.) contrast with office paraphernalia. In the end matter takes over and infiltrates the intimacy of the human body in order to glaze it into standard forms. It is the longest of the six poems (some hundred words), with long drawn-out verse-lines, neither stanzas nor rhyme. It shows a high degree of lexical and semantic cohesion. Parallelism is apparent in that it contains two sentences only, each of which carries a chain of very similar noun phrases in its trail.

Inventory of FG devices

I. PHONOLOGY
Statistical Deviation:
- the consonant clusters in lines 8, 9
- /e/ in line 1
- /uː/ in line 11
- /eɪ/ in line 13
- /n/ and /s/ in line 1
- /p/ in lines 2, 7
- /l/ in lines 3, 4
- /m/ in line 3
- /ʃ/ in lines 4, 5
- /r/ in line 5
- /k/ in lines 7, 8
- /v/ and /ʃ/ in lines 8, 9
- /t/ in line 11
- /d/ in line 13
- /g/ in line 13

Determinate Deviation:
- extra stress on lexical items: 'sadness', 'dolour', 'misery', 'pathos', 'ritual', 'alive', 'duplication', 'afternoons'

Internal Deviation:
- monosyllables in line 9
- 'institutions' against monosyllables in line 9
- /ɪə/ in line 11 ⎱
- /ʊə/ in line 7 ⎰ : only observed cases
- lines 6, 9: do not begin with stressed syllable
- line 6: anapaestic amidst dactylic lines
- spondees in final three lines

Parallelism:
- places/faces (line 4, 13)
- assonance:
  - inexorable-pencils
  - paperweight
  - misery-manila- mucilage
  - desolation-places

                    - pathos-basin
                    - paperclip-duplication
                    - finer-alive
                    - silica-sift-invisible
                    - fine-eyebrows
                    - film-delicate-duplicate
                    - glazing-pale-faces
        -       delicate/duplicate (lines 12, 13)
        -       alliterations:
                line (1)   inexorable - known - neat
                line (2)   pad - paperweight
                line (3)   misery - manila - mucilage
                line (4)   public - places
                line (5)   lonely - lavatory/reception room
                line (6/7)   pathos - pitcher (paperclip)
                line (7)   clip - comma
                line (10)   finer - flour/silica - sift
                line (12)   fine - film
                line (13)   pale - duplicate/glazing - grey/
                                duplicate - standard
        -       parallelism between spondees in lines 12, 13

II. GRAMMAR
Statistical Deviation:
                none
Determinate Deviation:
        -       selection restriction violations in lines 1, 2, 3, 6, 7, 8
        -       'alive' (line 10)
        -       'glazing' (line 13)
        -       'duplicate faces' (line 13)
Internal Deviation:
        -       'and': only conjunction in line 9
        -       lines 8, 13: end to enumeration
        -       present participles in lines 12, 13
Parallelism:
        -       lines 1, 9
        -       all NPs are patterned
        -       dropping/glazing (lines 12, 13)
        -       modifiers of 'dust': 'finer', 'alive', 'dangerous', 'invisible'
        -       singular head-words in object-NPs vs. plural elaborations.

III. SEMANTICS
Statistical Deviation:
                'rare' words: 'multigraph', 'pitcher', 'mucilage', 'manila',
                'pathos',   'silica',   'tedium',   'dolour',   ('desolation',
                'immaculate',   'ritual',   'duplication',   'institution',
                'inexorable', 'invisible', 'duplicate', 'delicate').
Internal Deviation:
        -       'known', 'seen' in lines 1, 9 (against the dominance of nouns
                and adjectives)
        -       'body' words in lines 12, 13

-         'grey' in line 13 (only colour word)
-         line 9: introduction of new topic after long enumeration

Determinate Deviation:
        none

Parallelism:
-         contrast two main verbs (lines 1, 9) with present participles (lines 12, 13)
-         contrast ABSTRACT - CONCRETE nouns
  conrast HUMAN   - -HUMAN nouns
-         'duplication' (line 8) - 'duplicate' (line 13) and indirectly: 'standard' (line 13) - 'multigraph' (line 7)
-         'finer' (line 10) - 'fine' (line 12)
-         opposition everyday words - technical vocabulary

FIG. 3.3 VISUAL REPRESENTATION OF FG IN ROETHKE'S POEM

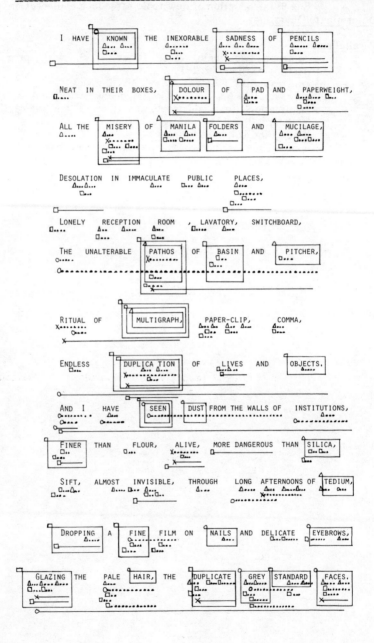

TABLE 3.3 PREDICTIONS: ROETHKE

Ranks given to lines

Line	Rank
1	2
2	4
3	5
4	12
5	13
6	7
7	8
8	3
9	6
10	11
11	10
12	9
13	1

Division of lines
FG: 1, 2, 3, 8, 9, 13
MG: 6, 7, 11, 12
BG: 4, 5, 10

'Mirage' by Christina Rossetti[4]

1   The hope I dreamed of was a dream,

2   Was but a dream; and now I wake,

3   Exceeding comfortless, and worn and old,

4   For a dream's sake.

5   I hang my harp upon a tree,

6   A weeping willow in a lake;

7   I hang my silenced harp there, wrung and snapt,

8   For a dream's sake.

9   Lie still, lie still, my breaking heart;

10   My silent heart, lie still and break,

11   Life, and the world, and mine own self, are changed

12   For a dream's sake.

The poem by Christina Rossetti displays the traditional form more than any other poem in the sample. It shows least FG in terms of deviations, but contains a high amount of parallelism, in which, however, exact repetition is higher than in any other of the poems. It is built around a central theme of lost hope, and has a typically preraphaelite, dreamy atmosphere. It has very little to offer in terms of new experience of the world, and is perhaps the weakest of the poems employed.

Inventory of FG devices

I. PHONOLOGY
Statistical Deviation:
- /iː/ in line 1
- /æ/ in line 7
- /aɪ/ in lines 9-11
- /aː/ in stanza III
- consonants:
  /m/ in line 1
  /w/ in lines 2, 6
  /p/ and /h/ in line 5
  /s/, /p/, /h/, and /ŋ/ in line 7
  /n/ and /f/ in line 11.
  /t/ and /l/ in lines 9,10

Determinate Deviation:
  none

Internal Deviation:
- /e/ and /ɜː/ in line 11
- /ɛə/ and /aʊ/ in lines 2,7
- line 3: considerably less monosyllables than in other lines
- only affricates in line 1
- slight enjambements in lines 7, 11
- reversed stress pattern in line 11

Parallelism:
- rhymes on /eɪ/
- assonance:

/iː /	in:	dreamed, dream (line 1); dream (lines 2, 4); exceeding (line 3)
/æ /	in:	hang (line 5); snapt, hang (line 7)
/aɪ /	in:	I, silenced (line 7); lie, lie, silent, lie, life, mine (lines 9-11)
/aː/	in:	harp (lines 5, 7); heart (line 9)
/eɪ /	in:	break (line 10); changed (line 11)

- alliteration:
  hang - harp (lines 5, 7)
  willow - weeping (line 6)

II GRAMMAR
Statistical Deviation:

Determinal Deviation:
   no conjunction reductions in lines 3, 11
Internal Deviation:
   - no ADJ + ADJ in line 11
   - no SVO structure in line 1
   - no fronting of ADV in line 11
   - imperatives in lines 9 and 10
   - only plural verb (and subject) in line 11
   - line 1 in past tense
Parallelism:
   - patterning of imperatives in lines 9 and 10
   - ADJ + ADJ in lines 3, 7
   - 'my' + ADJ + N in lines 7, 9, 10, 11
   - patterning of elements in subject of line 11
   - 'I hang my harp' in lines 5, 7
   - syntactic patterning around 'dream' in lines 1, 2
   - recurring present participles in lines 3, 6, 9
   - recurring past participles in lines 3, 7, 11
   - contrast between tenses in lines 1, 2

III. SEMANTICS
Statistical Deviation:
   - lexical items: 'wrung', 'snapt', 'mine', 'exceeding'
   - line 5 (hang harp in tree)
Determinate Deviation:
   none
Internal Deviation:
   - 'the' in lines 1 and 11
   - nouns in third stanza do not correspond to the feature pattern of stanza I and II
Parallelism:
   contrast 'was' - 'now' in line 1

IV. CONCLUSION
The previous observations lead one to conclude that most of the FG devices in the poem are located in lines 1, 9, 10, 11, while the BG is formed by lines 4, 5, 8 and 12. For what lies in between, the decisions seem much more difficult to make, even with the help of the visual representation. Perhaps we may say that lines 2 and 3 are more in the FG, while lines 6 and 7 belong more to the BG.

FIG. 3.4 VISUAL REPRESENTATION OF FG IN ROSSETTI'S POEM

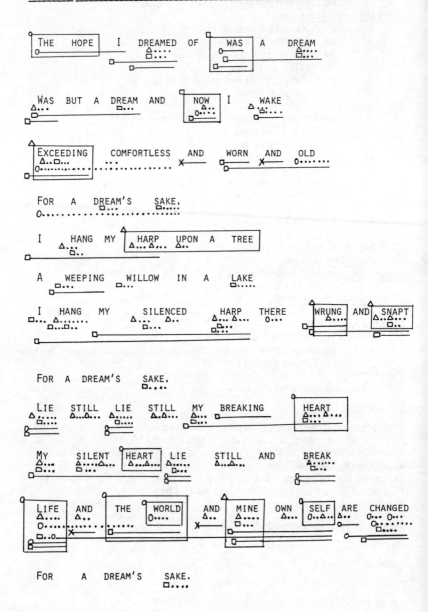

TABLE 3.4 PREDICTIONS: ROSSETTI

Rank given to lines

Line	Rank
1	3
2	5
3	6
4	10
5	9
6	7
7	8
8	11
9	1
10	4
11	2
12	12

Division of lines
FG: 1, 9, 10, 11
MG: 2, 3, 6, 7
BG: 4, 5, 8, 12

'Was there a time' by Dylan Thomas[5]

1   Was there a time when dancers with their fiddles

2   In children's circuses could stay their troubles?

3   There was a time they could cry over books,

4   But time has set its maggot on their track.

5   Under the arc of the sky they are unsafe.

6   What's never known is safest in this life.

7   Under the skysigns they who have no arms

8   Have cleanest hands, and, as the heartless ghost

9   Alone's unhurt, so the blind man sees best.

The fifth text selected is a lesser known poem by Dylan Thomas on the theme of lost childhood. The opening lines are very evocative of childhood but not very foregrounded, and lead to a series of generic statements that are highly paradoxical, pointing to a reversal of normal values in human life. The poem has no stanzas or rhyme, but contains highly original metaphorical language. There is not much parallelism in this text, and the main FG effects hinge on the deviational aspect, which takes the form of paradoxes.

Inventory of FG devices

I. PHONOLOGY
Statistical Deviation:
- contracted forms: 'what's' and 'alone's'
- vowel distribution:
  /aɪ/ in line 3
  /æ/ in line 4
  /ʌ/, /ɑː/ and /eɪ/ in line 5
  /uː/ and /aɪ/ in line 7
  /æ/ in line 8
  /əʊ/ in line 9
- consonant distribution:
  /w/ and /z/ in line 1
  /z/ in lines 2, 7, 8 and 9
  /k/ in line 3
  /t/, /m/ and /g/ in line 4
  /ð/ in line 5
  /n/, /s/ and /f/ in line 6
  /h/ in lines 7, 8
  /s/, /l/ and /g/ in line 8
  /n/, /s/, /l/ and /b/ in line 9

Determinate Deviation:
  none

Internal Deviation:
- enjambement in lines 1-2, 7-8, and 8-9
- defeated metrical expectancies: lines 1, 3, 5, 7, 9
- opposition between metre and rhythm
  - first two words
  - with (line 1)
  - could, over (line 3)
  - on (line 4)
  - in (line 6)
  - as (line 8)
- consonant clusters in lines 1, 2, 7, 8, 9
- 'safest' carrying stress in line 6

Parallelism:
- consonantal 'rhymes' in lines 1, 2, 3, 5, 6, 8, and 9
- assonance:
  line (1): fiddles, children's, circuses, with
  line (3): could, books
  line (4): has, maggot, track
  line (5): they, unsafe
  line (8): have, hands, and, (man)
  line (9): ghost, alone's, so
- alliteration:
  line (3): could, cry
  line (6): never, known

line (7): sky<u>s</u>igns
line (7): <u>wh</u>o <u>h</u>ave;
line (8): <u>h</u>ave, <u>h</u>ands, <u>h</u>eartless
line (9): <u>b</u>lind, <u>b</u>est
-       /aɪ/ rhymes in all lines (except 2 and 8)

II. GRAMMAR
Statistical Deviation:
-       the use of 'stay' in line 2
-       the postponement of the VP in line 2
Determinate Deviation:
    none
Internal Deviation:
-       the change to present perfect tense in line 4
-       the change to present simple tense in line 5
-       the first full verb in line 9
-       no PP in line 9
-       enjambements in lines 1, 7, 8
-       conjunctions in lines 4, 8, 9
-       sentences 3 and 4 do not contain embeddings
Parallelism:
-       PP in sentences 4 and 6: 'under the X'
-       two PP in sentence 1
-       DET ADJ IN V ADJ in sentence 7
-       'there' in sentences 1 and 2
-       question/answer structure of sentences 1 and 2, and syntactic mirroring in sentences 1 and 2: <u>be a time when X</u>

III. SEMANTICS
Statistical Deviation:
-       'maggot' in line 4: low predictability
-       ambiguity of 'their'
Determinate Deviation:
-       'skysigns' (neologism)
-       selection restriction violation in line 4: time/set, time/maggot, maggot/track
-       violations of truth conditions in lines 7-9
Internal Deviation:
-       'see' in line 9: first full verb conjugated
-       'safest': first adjective
-       '<u>the</u>' arc: first homophoric reference
-       '<u>the</u> heartless ghost': first cataphoric reference
-       'cleanest': no definite article
-       first instance of generic 'they' in line 7
Parallelism:
-       recurrence of 'time', 'safe', 'sky'
-       oppositions: safest/unsafe, arms/hands, blind/sees/best
-       relations between superlatives of adjectives: safest, cleanest, best
-       argumentative meaning aspects in conjunctions 'as', 'so'

FIG. 3.5 VISUAL REPRESENTATION OF FG IN THOMAS' POEM

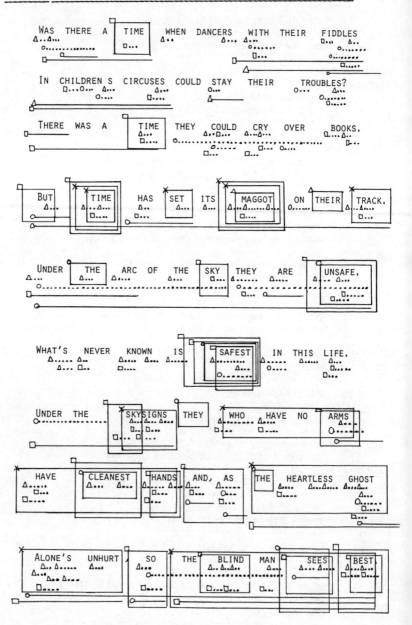

TABLE 3.5 PREDICTIONS: THOMAS

Ranks given to lines

Line	Rank
1	9
2	8
3	7
4	2
5	6
6	5
7	3
8	4
9	1

Division of lines
FG: 4, 7, 8, 9
MG: 5, 6,
BG: 1, 2, 3

'On the Banks of a Rocky Stream' by William Wordsworth[6]

1 Behold an emblem of our human mind

2 Crowded with thoughts that need a settled home

3 Yet, like to eddying balls of foam

4 Within this whirlpool, they each other chase

5 Round and round, and neither find

6 An outlet nor a resting-place!

7 Stranger, if such disquietude be thine,

8 Fall on thy knees and sue for help divine.

The poem by Wordsworth is very short, and typical of his nature poetry, although the stream is seen here as an image of the human mind. Its romantic and pantheistic overtones may be readily perceived by a modern reader. Syntactically it is the most complex of the poems, and the deviational aspects of its FG are situated mainly on the semantic/pragmatic plane, while the parallelism is most obvious on the phonological level.

Inventory of FG devices

I. PHONOLOGY
Statistical Deviation:
- they, chase (line 4)
- round, round; neither, find (line 5)
  outlet, place (line 6)
- round and round and neither find (line 5)
- emblem, human, mind (line 1)
- within, this, they, other, each, chase (line 4)
- on, knees, and, divine (line 8)

Determinate Deviation:
  none

Internal Deviation:
- enjambements of lines 4 and 5, 5 and 6
- trochaic variations:
  'crowded' (line 2)
  line 5: (completely)
  'stranger' (line 7)
  'fall on' (line 8)
- spondee: 'yet like' (line 3)
- high regularity of leading syllables in line 8
- consonant cluster in 'stranger' (line 7)

Parallelism:
- behold/home/foam (lines 1, 2, 3)
- round/outlet (lines 5, 6)
- disquietude/thine/thy/divine (lines 7, 8)
- mind/find (lines 1, 5)
- chase/place (lines 4, 6)
- behold/human/(home) (line 1)
- within/whirlpool (line 4)
- round/round/(resting) (line 5)

II. GRAMMAR
Statistical Deviation:
- 'balls of foam' (normally: 'bubbles')
- 'help divine' (word-order)
- 'be' (line 8: subjunctive)
- 'thine', 'thy', (lines 7-8)

Determinate Deviation:
  none

Internal Deviation:
- 'if'-sentence in line 8 (against tense of other lines)
- fronting of embedded clause in line 7
- 'thine' in line 7 is first explicit mention of second person
  pronoun

Parallelism:
- 'our' (line 1) contrast with 'thine' (line 7) and 'thy' (line 8)
- 'behold/fall': syntactically and typographically
- 'human mind/help divine'
- 'fall/sue': imperatives in line 8

-     'thoughts': DS subject of different sentences
-     'fall on your knees' parallel with 'sue for help divine'

III. SEMANTICS
Statistical Deviation:
-     archaisms: be, sue, behold, emblem, thine, thy, like to

Determinate Deviation:
-     selection restriction violation: <u>mind crowded</u>
-     selection restriction violation: <u>thoughts</u> that need a settled <u>home</u>

Internal Deviation:
-     'divine': religious theme introduced
-     'stranger': conative aspect stressed
-     'our': only generic pronoun
-     'this' (line 4): only exophoric reference
-     'such' (line 7): only back-pointing deictic

Parallelism:
-     'human mind/help divine'
-     'behold/fall'
-     'human, eddying/divine, settled'
-     anaphoric relationship between 'emblem' and the title

IV. CONCLUSIONS
In this poem by Wordsworth, both beginning and final lines constitute the FG, while the middle lines form the BG. (Because of the low number of lines in this poem, it was decided not to include a MG category in this division.) The division is also interesting from quite an unexpected point of view. The BG lines show more marked phonological patterning, while the FG lines contain more grammatical and semantic devices. Thus the poem can be used to test to some extent the general assumption about the relative weightings to be given to the different linguistic layers, i.e. phonology, grammar, semantics.

FIG. 3.6 VISUAL REPRESENTATION OF FG IN WORDSWORTH'S POEM

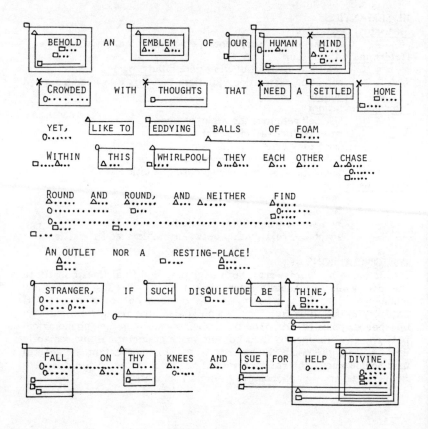

TABLE 3.6 PREDICTIONS: WORDSWORTH

Ranks given to lines

Line	Rank
1	4
2	2
3	8
4	7
5	6
6	5
7	3
8	1

Division of lines
FG: 1, 2, 7, 8
BG: 1, 4, 5, 6

NOTES

1. See Cummings (1960: 64). For a more detailed treatment of this poem, see Van Peer (forthcoming).
2. See Dickinson (1968: 40).
3. See Roethke (1957: 55).
4. See Rossetti (1904:350).
5. See Thomas (1971: 59).
6. See Wordsworth (1977: 902).

Chapter Four

THE VALIDITY OF FOREGROUNDING

INTRODUCTION

To facilitate the discussion, the empirical data have been listed in Appendix 2. The reader can consult the tables containing the raw data there; reference to them is only made when it is in the interest of clarity. In general the data for each hypothesis are discussed separately, first of all across the poems used in the experiments generally. The results for separate poems or for different subgroups will then follow.

For the hypotheses tested with the help of data in the nominal scale of measurements (i.e. results from Part B, C, E and F) the distribution of frequencies in both FG and BG categories was first tabulated. For the memory test this meant: the number of right recalls versus wrong (or no) recall, for the underlining test it meant the number of times each word had been underlined (or not). These frequencies were grouped per verse-line and separated into two classes, FG and BG, according to the analyses shown in the previous chapter. Care had been taken to make the two classes approximately equal in the numbers of items they contained, and where unequal, the BG category was given the benefit. The following table shows this distribution:

The validity of foregrounding

Table 4.1. Proportion of FG/BG text-elements

		FG	BG + MG
Part B:	No. of items deleted	15	15
Part C, E:	No. of lines	20	26
	No. of words	141	146

HYPOTHESIS ONE: MEMORABILITY

The distribution of correct and wrong recalls may be found in <u>Appendix 2B</u>. Together with the z-values of the binomial test, the x^2-values and the associated probability-values are found in the following table.

Table 4.2. Memorability: Binomial and x^2-tests

	z	p	x^2	p
Cummings	– 3.67	.05	39.28	.001
Dickinson	– 3.19	.04	27.46	.001
Roethke	– 5.85	.00003	69.79	.001
Thomas	– 3.82	.00007	9.54	.01

The z-values listed in <u>Table 4.2</u> result from the binomial test, indicating the probability with which the distribution over the dichotomy FG/BG is associated. x^2-values indicate the relationship between the categories FG/BG on the one hand, and right or wrong recalls on the other hand. As the table shows, all analyses of the data yielded results that are significant below the level of $\alpha <$ .05. A close inspection of the data listed in <u>Appendix 2B</u> however reveals that these significant results by themselves are misleading: in the poem by Thomas, the difference in recall between FG and BG items is significant <u>in the opposite direction</u> to the one predicted, i.e. BG items are recalled significantly better than FG ones.

The conclusion from the memory test is therefore obvious: the null-hypothesis cannot be rejected in all cases. As this is only possible with three of the poems used, the predictions about the effect of FG on memory as derived from the theory must at this stage be refuted: no empirical evidence suggests that its truth should be upheld. As pointed out in Chapter 2 such negative results are not readily interpretable from the data. The question therefore is whether the prediction derived from the theory is not an accurate measure for the theory itself, for instance because of the interference in memory processing of other variables, which may have little or nothing to do with the qualities of FG. It is known from memory research, for instance, that concrete nouns are generally recalled more easily than abstract ones. Thus in the Cummings poem the BG item 'violets' would be _easier_ to recall (something which was indeed borne out by the pilot-test). Words at the beginning and at the end of the text could also be more easily remembered than words in the middle, because of primacy and recency effects. Words that rhyme are also easier to recall, because of the extra redundancy introduced, thereby creating differences in ease of recall between FG caused by parallelism and that originating in deviance. It should also be remembered that the design of the memory test had some drawbacks too: it combines memorability with a cloze-procedure, which allows for extrapolation on the basis of grammatical structure and contextual information. Consequently the recall task must have been influenced by general expectancy. This contamination of different variables, together with the lack of experimental control over some of them, makes it impossible to dissociate the real cause(s) from concurring factors. Presumably the rather naive view that had been taken of memorability and the somehow superficial analogy to the 'Von Restorff'-effect may account for the contradictory results observed in the data. Further research, in which other factors influencing ease of memorability are systematically controlled by the experimenter, is needed to arrive at more conclusive evidence. In the light of what is known about the multitude of variables influencing recall, however, the design of such empirical tests will not be an easy matter.

HYPOTHESIS TWO: STRIKINGNESS

This postulate was tested through Part C of the experiment: Appendix 2C summarizes the number of underlinings for different verse-lines in the various poems. As may be seen the predictions of H_2 are borne out in a systematic way: in all four poems the total number of underlined words is considerably higher for the FG lines than those belonging to the BG. The binomial test reveals whether these differences are large enough to be statistically significant. The χ^2-test investigates the relationship between on the one hand words being underlined or not underlined in the responses and their belonging to either the FG or BG category.

Table 4.3. Strikingness: Binomial and χ^2-tests.

	z	p	χ^2	p
Cummings	- 14.36	.00003	248.10	.001
Dickinson	- 2.47	.0068	17.38	.001
Roethke	- 4.62	.00003	44.00	.001
Thomas	- 5.17	.00003	70.61	.001

As may be seen in Table 4.3, the difference in frequency of underlined words between FG/BG lines as indicated by the binomial test is highly significant in all four poems. Simultaneously Ss' decision to underline words or not is significantly associated to the FG/BG division: this may be derived from the systematically high significance of the χ^2-values. The results consistently confirm the predictions made in H_2 with respect to the strikingness of FG. Hence it seems safe, at least for the time being, to accept these results as confirming the theoretical model with respect to the strikingness-value of FG configurations in poetry.

HYPOTHESIS THREE: IMPORTANCE

The rankings allocated to randomized phrases or to verse-lines from the poem may be found in Appendix 2D. The average rank for each phrase was calculated and then matched to the predicted ranks given at the end of the stylistic analysis of each of the poems (see Chapter 3). The Spearman rank correlations for this comparison, together with their associated p-values, are listed in the following table:

Table 4.4. Importance: Spearman rank correlation

	N	r_s	p
Cummings	12	.90	.01
Dickinson	9	.90	.01
Roethke	9	.78	.01
Thomas	9	.90	.01

As can be seen, three of the coefficents are very high (.90) and all p-values are highly significant. Considering the difficulties in making accurate predictions for the ranking of verse-lines and the risk involved, it is fair to say that these results offer strong support for the theory. Hence H_0 must be rejected and H_3 accepted. In other words, there is serious ground to accept the idea that stretches of text belonging to the FG are felt to be more 'important' than passages that are part of the BG or MG of the text.

HYPOTHESIS FOUR: DISCUSSION VALUE

Part E of the experiments investigated the discussion-value of different stretches of text. The nominal data obtained in the test are listed in Appendix 2E. The binomial test was carried out first, to find out whether any differences in frequencies in underlining between FG and BG lines of the poem were significant. The χ^2-test shows the strength of association between Ss' decision to underline (or not) and the FG/BG dichotomy. This is shown in the following table:

Table 4.5. Discussion Value. Binomial and x^2-tests

	$\underline{z}$	$\underline{p}$	$\underline{x^2}$	$\underline{p}$
Cummings	- 14.34	.00003	195.07	.001
Dickinson	- 9.10	.00003	234.03	.001
Roethke	- 7.84	.00003	112.72	.001
Thomas	- 4.97	.00003	63.52	.001

As Table 4.5 shows, for each of the four texts used in the experiment, the difference in underlinings between FG and BG lines are significant at a very low level of probability, hence confirming the predictions in a powerful way: each p-value is far below the level indicated, since p equals .00003 for z = 4.00. Furthermore, the x^2-results indicate a highly significant effect of the IV on the DV. In other words, Ss' response (underline the item or not) strongly relates to the fact that the item under consideration belongs to either FG or BG of the poem. Notice that in each of these cases the x^2-values are a long way above the required value for a probability of p = .001, which is $x^2 = 10.83$.

HYPOTHESIS FIVE: INDIVIDUALITY

Since the theory of foregrounding assumes some general consensus of reader response to poetry, this assumption needs separate testing. Falsification in this case would detract from the support found in favour of the theoretical model, while confirmation would further add to the strength of the previous hypotheses. To this end the x^2-test was used as a goodness-of-fit test for the nominal data. This technique inspects whether the amount of agreement found in the data is large enough to allow an experimenter the conclusion that there is overall consistency in Ss' responses. Significant p-values indicate that the consensus between informants is larger than could have been expected on the basis of chance alone. The x^2 -values, together with their p-values, are listed below for the different tests:

Table 4.6.
Intersubjectivity (Part B, C, E): x^2 -test of goodness-of-fit

	x^2	df	p
Part B			
Cummings	19.39	5	.001/.01
Dickinson	38.71	5	.001
Roethke	101.45	9	.001
Thomas	17.00	7	.01/.02
Part C			
Cummings	438.95	11	.001
Dickinson	198.99	11	.001
Roethke	202.05	12	.001
Thomas	281.63	8	.001
Part E			
Cummings	458.38	11	.001
Dickinson	293.53	11	.001
Roethke	231.68	12	.001
Thomas	246.37	8	.001

As may be seen from Table 4.6, the analysis strongly confirms predictions. Note that the level of significance of 5% is passed with an extremely wide margin. For the p-value to be below .05, a x^2 -value of only 19.68 was needed for df = 11 (i.e. for the first three poems in the tables). Values that run in hundreds, as above, have probabilities that are far below the value cited (i.e. .001). Hence the support provided by the data in favour of a general consensus among Ss, is quite strong.

It is important to point out in this respect that these findings were replicated in Part F, which was run during a later experiment. There, the x^2 as goodness-of-fit test yielded the following results:

Table 4.7.
Intersubjectivity (Part F): x^2 -test of goodness-of-fit

	x^2	df	p
Dickinson	338.30	11	.001
Thomas	192.22	8	.001
Wordsworth	62.64	7	.001

Notice how the probabilities are again _far_ below the required 5% level. Hence these later tests offer further ground for confirmation of the hypothesis. At the same time, they corroborate the reliability of the previously acquired results.

For data measured in the ordinal scale the appropriate test to be used is the Kendall Coefficient of Concordance. This coefficient is matched to a X^2-distribution in order to inspect the associated probability. Both of these statistical measures are listed in the following table:

Table 4.8
Intersubjectivity (Part D): Kendall's Coefficient of Concordance W

	W	X^2	df	p
Cummings	.52	275.6	11	.001
Dickinson	.38	141.8	8	.001
Roethke	.44	169.0	8	.001
Thomas	.38	148.3	8	.001

As can be read from the table, the level of consensus between informants occurs at a low probability. These results may again be compared to the ordinal data collected in _Part F_:

Table 4.9
Intersubjectivity (Part F): Kendall's Coefficient of Concordance W

	W	X^2	df	p
Dickinson	.55	121.26	11	.001
Thomas	.28	51.72	8	.001
Wordsworth	.20	32.71	7	.001

Again the intersubjective amount of agreement in this experiment strongly confirms the earlier support for the theory. It seems inevitable, in the light of this evidence in favour of H_5, that H_0 must be rejected and that we must accept the data as a warrant for the theory that readers conceive of text passages as entities which can be rank-ordered along a continuum of importance, or which can be treated as possessing discussion value or strikingness. The degree of consensus between individual Ss guarantees that the outcome of the analyses cannot merely be attributed to chance effects.

HYPOTHESIS SIX: COHESION

The assumption that FG works in a coherent way, and that FG passages thereby contribute most to an interpretation of the poem, was tested in Part F. The task set to informants was of a dual nature, but both tasks were geared towards considerations of what Ss found essential in the text for the sake of interpreting it. In the first part of the experiment, and after they had read an introductory page explaining what they were meant to understand by 'interpretation', they were asked to underline those passages in the text that they thought contributed most to their construction of an interpretation of it. There was no limit on the number of things Ss could underline, nor on the length of what they could consider as a meaningful unit of text, and they were told so explicitly before the experiment started. There were no questions or remarks on the part of the Ss, although they were invited to do so by the experimenter, and the task seemed to be a meaningful one to them. In a second part of the test they were asked to rank-order the verse-lines of the poem in decreasing order of importance for this construction of an interpretation. Since the results of this test are not so clear as for the previous ones, more time must be spent on verbal analysis and discussion in this section.

The nominal data provided by the underlining test will be investigated with the help of a binomial test first:

Table 4.10 Cohesion/Interpretation: Binomial test

	z	p
Dickinson	- 7.12	.00003
Thomas	- .20	.4207
Wordsworth	- 4.32	.00003

As can be seen in the table, both the Dickinson and the Wordsworth poem yield highly significant results. This can be translated in terms of the experiment by saying that the difference in underlinings between the two categories under scrutiny (i.e. FG and BG) shows up in a highly significant degree and in the direction predicted. Consequently, Ss perceived of FG and BG as two different categories, thereby confirming the conclusions of previous experiments.

If one looks at the results of the Thomas poem, however, one notices that the underlinings in both categories are near to equal (the balance tips slightly over to the BG side); this resulted in a p-value of .42, indicating the lack of any significant difference between the two categories. Closer investigation reveals that the reason for this departure from our predictions lies in the enormous accumulation of underlinings in line 6, which is a 'middle ground' line according to the stylistic analysis. If one removes line 6 the test becomes highly significant, with $z = -7.28$ and $p < .00003$ (while the total number of FG and BG lines and words in that case still remains equal). If we turn back to the underlining tests of the previous experiment, something similar may be observed. In these experiments line 6 of the Thomas poem attracted a considerably higher number of underlinings than was expected. This departure from our predictions is too systematic to let the case go unnoticed.

In the analysis line 6 was predicted as possessing low FG on the basis of the fact that:

(a)   it does not show any kind of significant deviation in terms of its phonology, grammar or semantics;

(b)   it is not conspicuously parallel with some other part of the text.

However, if one had to indicate verse-lines that sum up the whole poem best then the last part of line 9 ('the blind man sees best') and line 6 are likely candidates. In view of the fact that the first part of line 9 ('Alone's unhurt') is not very relevant to a summary of the poem, it could be the case that line 6 is all the more appealing in this respect. (Unfortunately we have no data on the memorability of items in line 6: in the memory test no items from it were included, precisely on the ground that it occupies neither a strong FG nor a far BG position). Although one could argue that line 6 displays some kind of internal deviation, since it is the first in a series of generic statements of a paradoxical nature (also containing the first of a series of superlatives), this by itself does not seem a sufficient explanation for its high status in Ss' preferences. What may be the case rather, is the fact that in the process of interpreting a poem, some aspects of thematic structure may override aspects of FG. In other words, the hierarchical information structure in a text may (or may not) contrast with the hierarchical structure of FG in a poem. In the other poems it appears that the FG hierarchy matched the thematic hierarchy fairly well. In the Thomas poem however, there seems to be a mismatch between the FG and the thematic hierarchy. This may be represented as follows:

Table 4.11
FG and thematic hierarchy in the poem by Thomas

Rank	Lines in FG hierarchy	Lines in Thematic hierarchy
1	9	6
2	4	9
3	7	4
4	8	7
5	6	8

If the previous argumentation holds, then reference to the difference between prominence and (motivated) FG, as made by Halliday (1971), forces itself on the analysis. The notion of motivation may be system-atized in a more meaningful way if it is linked to the 'macro-structure' of the text; see Van Dijk (1977: 6). Although not much is as yet known about the specific nature of such macro-units and the way they inter-act with lower level units and stylistic or rhetorical devices, there seems to be some ground to accept their existence; see, for instance, Van Dijk (1980). The data for the Thomas poem appear to indicate a disparity between its thematic structure and its FG organization. Line 6 then should be seen as coming closer to a macro-structure than other lines, while these other lines contain more instances of FG. Further research will be necessary, though, to validate this point. Especially poems with good 'summary' lines and without much FG, but displaying a high amount of FG in other lines, are good candidates for empirical testing.

To return to the data of Part F, these can also be subjected to a χ^2-test of association. The following table summarizes the results of this test.

Table 4.12
Cohesion/Interpretation: χ^2 goodness-of-fit

	χ^2	p
Dickinson	188.79	.001
Thomas	29.20	.001
Wordsworth	2.67	.10/.20 (p= .10 for χ^2 = 2.71)

As can be seen, both the Dickinson and the Thomas poem yield highly significant results, indicating a strong relationship between FG on the one hand and the reader's decision to underline a particular passage in the poem on the other hand. For Wordsworth the p-value comes close to 10%, hence surpassing the level of rejection of H_0. Inspection of Appendix 2F reveals that the strongest deviation from the predictions is found for line 6, which, although of a BG nature, in terms of percentage of underlinings per word has the highest proportion of underlinings in the whole poem: 79% of its words are underlined (62% only for line 8, which comes next). A similar deviation from the predictions is found in line 7 which, although being FG according to our analysis, only gets marginally more underlined words than some lines which are BG. One possible interpretation is that the very end of the syntactically complex sentence in line 6 attracts attention, and not, as had been predicted, the beginning of a new sentence. Another possiblity lies in the fact that in this poem the division between the number of words in the FG and in the BG categories is biased in favour of the FG. In all other poems, care had been taken to divide the lines and words in such a way that the odds of the underlinings would be against the predictions. However in the poem by Wordsworth this is hard to do. If one looks at the number of words in the FG and BG one finds that there are 30 and 24 respectively. If one includes line 1, which of all FG lines comes closest to the BG, into the BG classes, the distribution of words in both classes becomes:

FG : 23 words

BG : 31 words.

If one applies this new categorization to the test results, $x^2 = 5.07$ for df = 1; p is then situated between .02 and .05, hence a significant result indicating a strong association between FG and underlining.

Could it be that in this case the thematic structure interferes, as in the Thomas poem? This seems unlikely, as the first two and last two lines seem to sum up the theme of the text much better than any line from the middle part. Moreover, line 6 cannot hold an extremely high position in the thematic hierarchy: it is very short (the shortest of the whole poem), it does not contain a verb, it needs line 5 to be syntactically and semantically well-formed, and is still situated in the simile.

Appendix 2F also lists the results of the second part of this experiment, in which Ss ranked verse-lines in decreasing order of importance for their construction of an interpretation of the text. The Spearman rank correlation test investigates the way in which the average ranks thus obtained match to the predicted ranks:

Table 4.13
Cohesion/Interpretation: Spearman rank correlation

	r_s	p
Dickinson	.68	.01/.05
Thomas	.61	.01/.05
Wordsworth	.81	.01/.05

As is clear from Table 4.13 the match between observed data and predictions is statistically significant in all cases. Considering the systematic nature of these significant results one may legitimately conclude that the data support the hypothesis derived from the theoretical model. The cohesive patterns of FG apparently make them play a prominent role in the cognitive processing of poems. At the same time the correlations cast some doubt over the insignificant results in the underlining test of Part F. Since the ranking test involves a higher risk for the predictions than the underlining test (because of the higher interdependence of data), these negative results are difficult to interpret meaningfully.

A tentative conclusion one may draw from Part F is that the predictions made on the basis of the stylistic analyses are in general borne out by the results. The major departures from the predictions can be interpreted as due to the fact that FG may interact with other structural principles of texts, for instance their thematic structure. Although in general there seems to be a strong tendency to have FG configurations in places that are also of high importance for the thematic structure, there may be cases where the two principles do not converge. Whether this detracts from the quality or from the effect of the poem remains difficult to say at the moment. In any case it is a possibility that the theory may have to allow for. An investigation of the interplay between the two principles may turn out to be of high value for the refinement of the notion of FG.

HYPOTHESIS SEVEN: REPEATED EXPOSURE

This hypothesis predicted that, since FG configurations act as interpretative signposts, repeated exposure to the text would heighten the degree of agreement between Ss, even if they had no opportunity to exchange opinions on this matter. Is it possible to examine the quantitative analyses of the data to this end? A growing consensus might show up in increasingly significant results of statistical analyses. One such opportunity presents itself, as the χ^2 as a goodness-of-fit test gives a measure of consensus amongst informants. Since we applied this to Parts B, C and E for all poems, we may expect an increase found for

χ^2 from B to C to E. This would indicate a higher amount of inter-subject agreement in Part E than in Part C, and a higher one in Part C than in Part B.

Table 4.14
Repeated exposure: goodness-of-fit

	Part B	Part C	Part E
Cummings	19.39	438.95	458.38
Dickinson	38.71	198.99	293.53
Roethke	101.45	202.05	231.68
Thomas	17.00	281.63	246.37

It is clear from Table 4.14 that there is a systematic increase in significance for each poem separately, except for the poem by Thomas, where a slight fall can be observed from Part C to Part E. Further confirmation of this tendency may be found in the performance of different subgroups. Inspection of these shows that, for every single poem used in the tests the number of significant results increases as the tests proceeded. In other words, the analysis of the data revealed that most of the insignificant results are found in Part B. However, the question should be asked whether the memory-test should not be considered as invalid, and hence left out of consideration here. In Part C, two insignificant results were observed, one only in Part D and none in Part E. Could this be attributed to the fact that informants became better at guessing our hidden aims? If this were to be the case, then Ss must have had a clearer expectancy of the design in the poems that were administered later in the experiment than in those that were administered first. Since the order of poems was not randomized in the first batch of experiments, it is possible to investigate this in an objective way. If one arranges the poems in the order in which all Ss were exposed to them (i.e. 1. Dickinson, 2. Cummings, 3. Roethke, 4. Thomas), the results of the poem by Thomas (the last one being administered) must be closer to our predictions than those of the poem by Dickinson (the very first one being read). Since the experimental procedure for each poem was exactly the same (a thing which can hardly have escaped Ss' attention), one would expect such a tendency to show up in the results. In a number of cases, however, quite the opposite can be observed, for instance, Part B results of the Thomas poem are considerably <u>less</u> significant than for the text by Emily Dickinson. So, in spite of the fact that Ss may have become increasingly familiar with the design it is not possible to show any clear effect of this in the data. Thus the increase in significant results cannot be attributed to familiarity with the procedures of the experiment. Instead I would like to suggest that the effect is due to repeated exposure to the texts themselves. Thus it may be postulated that the first exposure to a complex poem (especially if it is of a high degree of modernity) has a somewhat bewildering effect on the reader, the more so if he is not a trained reader of poetry. Repeated exposure allows him to detect the cohesive patterns of FG in the text that may be hard to grasp on a first reading. Thus Ss would gravitate towards a high degree of consensus on FG after repeated explorations of the text. Care should be taken, however, in interpreting these findings. Further research should be carried out in order to establish what processes a reader goes through after repeated exposure to the same text. Since this is an important issue, one would wish such research to be carried out in the future.

HYPOTHESIS EIGHT: SAMPLE VARIETY

The discussion of this hypothesis can be brief. In all analyses carried out and discussed so far, it has been noted that predictions were confirmed with all of the stimulus texts used. Such a systematic nature of confirmation adds further support to the theory. It should be noted that in the first series of test, poems were used which we felt would respond to FG analysis, as they contained overt linguistic oddity. One of these, i.e. the poem by Roethke, had been mentioned in a stylistic article - see Thorne (1970) - while the authors of two other poems (i.e. Cummings and Thomas) had also provided examples of FG which stylisticians had pointed to. The poem by Emily Dickinson was included to test the theory in the work of a poet who had not yet been mentioned in this connection, and who was of a totally different cultural and historical background. Later experiments, containing Part F, used two more poems. These were included mainly because they displayed less deviance. It is therefore all the more important to notice that in these more romantic poems too the predictions are in general borne out fairly well, at least if one accepts the refinement proposed in connection with the interaction between FG and thematic structure. It should be emphasized though that the degree of significance found with these 19th century poems (i.e. the ones by Rossetti and Wordsworth) tends to be somewhat lower than with the poems by modern authors. Compare, for instance, the z-values for the binomial test of the modern poems with those of the two 19th century poems; it is clear that the latter two have the lowest values:

Table 4.15
Sample variety: binomial test

	z
Cummings	-14.4
Dickinson	- 2.5
Roethke	- 4.6
Thomas	- 5.2
Wordsworth	- 4.3

(The values are those found in the analysis of Part C, except for the poem by Wordsworth, where it is the value of the Part F test). Although the tendency seems to be present, it should be emphasized that it is by no means very strong nor very systematic. For instance, the z-value is very high for the Dickinson poem in Part E. Similarly, no confirmation of the tendency can be found in the x^2-values; for instance the Dickinson poem yields a higher value in Part E than the modern poems. Thus although there seems to be some indication that the predictions work better with modern than with more traditional forms of poetry, this tendency cannot be said to detract from the general support in favour of the hypothesis that FG operates in a wide variety of lyrical texts.

HYPOTHESES NINE AND TEN: FAMILIARITY WITH THEORY, LITERARY TRAINING

These two hypotheses are treated together because they both deal with issues of the informants' formal training at university. The first one, i.e. H_9, bears on the subgroup of students having studied stylistics and hence being familiar with the theory of FG. The second one, H_{10}, refers to the subgroups of informants who have received a formal training in the study of literature, but who are not familiar with the theory of FG. In both cases the null-hypothesis should be accepted according to the theoretical model. The concrete predictions state that the differences in performance of the three subgroups of informants will not be significant at a statistical level of significance, and that on the other hand a significant association between the results of the three subgroups will be observed in the data. In the first place evidence will be provided in favour of the first postulate, i.e. that no significant difference exists between the results of the three subgroups. The nominal data of Part B through E are discussed to this end. The ordinal data will then follow, before turning to the opposite argumentation, i.e. that similarities between subgroups are significant.

The x^2 test of association can be used to this purpose. In this case the data (recalled items, underlined words) are cast into a 2 x 3 contingency table, the two horizontal rows containing the data for the FG and BG categories, while the three vertical columns contain the results of each subgroup. The x^2-test then shows whether a significant association between rows and columns exists. In other words, it shows whether the fact of belonging to one of the subgroups influences the reaction to FG or BG in the experimental task. The values of x^2 and their associated probabilities are tabulated below (for df = 2):

Table 4.16
Subgroups:χ^2-test

χ^2	Part B	Part C	Part E
Cummings	.187	2.50	7.33
Dickinson	.731	4.22	1.13
Roethke	.019	8.82	2.88
Thomas	.22	.27	3.21
p	Part B	Part C	Part E
Cummings	.90/.95	.20/.30	.01/.05
Dickinson	.50/.70	.10/.20	.50/.70
Roethke	.99	.01/.02	.20/.30
Thomas	.98/.99	.90/.80	.20/.30

The results speak for themselves: of the twelve tests carried out, only two are statistically significant. All other p-values fluctuate with a wide range, and three probabilities actually approach unity, indicating that the results are due to pure chance, or that absolutely no relation exists between subgroups and response type to either FG or BG. The two significant results may be interpreted as due to chance fluctuations.

It is perhaps warranted to digress for a moment here on the response given to the question whether Ss had actually read the poem before, or were familiar with its author. The results of these two questions are tabulated below.

Table 4.17
Recognition of text/author

	STY	ENG	NENG
Recognized the poem:	1 Cummings	3 Cummings	-
	6 Roethke	-	-
	1 Thomas	-	-
Recognized the poet:	9 Cummings	3 Cummings	-
	1 Thomas	-	-
	-	1 Dickinson	-

The validity of foregrounding

The picture emerging from <u>Table 4.17</u> is clear enough. Emily Dickinson has only been recognized once. Also the poem by Thomas was hard to recognize. However, the poem by Roethke was recognized by six Ss from the STY-group, while the one by Cummings was identified by ten stylistics students (out of 16) and by six literature students (out of 14). This confirms our expectations that informants from the STY-group could have been biased toward the texts, at least when compared with other subgroups. Notice that in the NENG-group not a single poem or poet had been recognized. Taking these differences into account, the amount of agreement between the three subgroups becomes all the more convincing.

Concerning the ordinal data obtained through Part D of the experiment, the question whether subgroups responded differently to the ranking task can be investigated through an appropriate statistic, the Kruskal-Wallis one-way analysis of variance. This technique calculates an H-value on the basis of the table of scores for each of the three independent conditions, in this case the three subgroups. The scores are then replaced by ranks, and the column totals provide the basis for the probability of difference in distribution. The concrete prediction in this case is that the probabilities associated with this difference in distribution are not significant, i.e. that subgroups do <u>not</u> differ significantly with respect to their variance in distribution.

Table 4.18
Subgroups: Kruskal-Wallis one-way analysis of variance

	$\underline{k}$	$\underline{n_j}$	$\underline{N}$	$\underline{df}$	$\underline{H}$	$\underline{p}$
Cummings	3	12	36	2	.012	.99
Dickinson	3	9	27	2	.054	.95/.98
Roethke	3	9	27	2	.014	.99
Thomas	3	9	27	2	.032	.98/.99

All p-values show extremely high values; in fact they all approach the value of $p = 1$. In other words, the probability of obtaining a similar distribution of ranks under the three different experimental conditions (i.e. the three independent subgroups in the sample) is almost equal to one. Or, the distribution of ranks in the three columns is as could be expected on the basis of chance. Consequently, there is no ground to reject H_0. This means that there are no significant differences in the observed rankings in each of the three subgroups. In fact the p-values are so high, and so close to unity, that they suggest quite the opposite.

From the previous analyses the conclusion may be drawn that it is not possible to find any significant and systematic difference in response to the poems. But can one detect any indications to the contrary, i.e. is it possible to demonstrate a high degree of agreement between the three subgroups? This question can be investigated with the help of the Friedman two-way analysis of variance. In this case every single item presented for ranking to the Ss is considered as a different condition. If the performance of the three subgroups in this would be independent of the conditions, they would cancel each other out, making the rank total about equal for each condition. If, however, subgroups seriously agree with each other in reaction to the items, then this will show in significant values of the statistical analysis.

Table 4.19·
Subgroups: Friedman two-way analysis of variance

	N	k	χ^2	df	p
Cummings	3	12	31.08	11	.001/.01
Dickinson	3	9	22.40	8	.001/.01
Roethke	3	9	21.04	8	.001/.01
Thomas	3	9	21.78	8	.001/.01

The results support the previous conclusions: all p-values are situated between .01 and .001. In other words, the three subgroups significantly agree in their response to the items presented to them in the ranking task. This was further confirmed when Spearman rank correlations between overall rankings of different subgroups were computed: all coefficients had p-values lower than .01 (except one, which was situated between .01 and .05). A t-test carried out for the poem by Cummings (where the number of items presented was larger than 10) revealed that p-values associated with the similarity in ranking was systematically below the level of .0005, hence showing an extremely high degree of correspondence between the rankings of the three subgroups.

Finally, in order to visually display the amount of agreement between subgroups, it is possible to plot the data in the form of graphs. The x-axis shows the frequencies of the underlinings or the average ranks obtained, while the y-axis represents the different lines of the poem, ordered according to decreasing amounts of FG found in the analyses. The mean response for each subgroup is what has been plotted. Two such graphs are represented on the following page. The first one has been selected because it is the graph which shows the least fit between subgroups, while the second one shows the highest amount of intergroup correspondence that can be detected in the graphs. Inspection of the polygons of every subgroup reveals that there are quantitative differences between the groups. However, differences in qualitative terms are considerably less conspicuous. This can be derived from the direction the graph takes after each point. The graph representing the best fit between groups does not contain one instance in which the polygons take different directions after a coordinate. The graph for the Roethke poem, which shows the worst inter-group fit of all graphs, contains several deviations for the NENG-group, while the STY- and ENG-groups roughly follow the same directions, except after rank 2 and rank 11, where the STY-group shoots upwards. The general pattern in the graphs however shows few such cases. There is also a tendency for the STY-group to occupy the topmost position, with the ENG-group under it and the NENG-group scoring lowest. This seems to indicate that Ss familiar with FG and stylistic analysis indicate more words as striking or possessing discussion value. The NENG-group, i.e. informants with no literary training at all, tends to indicate least items, with the ENG-group (students with literary training) situated in the middle. In general the valleys of the polygon made by the response of STY- and ENG-groups are also considerably deeper than those of the NENG-group. This could be explained as these informants' tendency to make sharper discriminations between what is striking and what is not.

Fig. 4.1 Roethke: Subgroups' frequency distribution

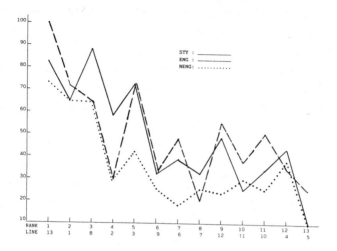

Fig. 4.2 Thomas: Subgroups' frequency distribution

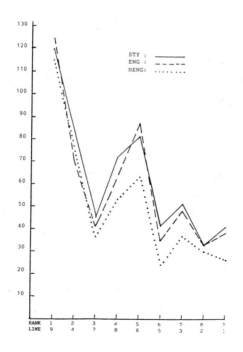

Note that this tendency can also be noticed in the ordinal data provided by Part D. There the average ranks of the STY-group come closer to the predicted ranks than those of the ENG-group, and these in turn come closer to predictions than the line representing the average rankings of the NENG-group. Yet these differences are a matter of degree, as most lines run fairly parallel. And as the previous analyses have shown, the differences are not statistically significant.

To conclude: both statistical analyses and graphs plotting average responses of subgroups reveal that with respect to H_9 and H_{10} the null-hypothesis should be accepted, as had been predicted. No systematic difference between subgroups can be established that is significant below the previously set level of $p < .05$. Instead the amount of correlation found between the three subgroups abundantly demonstrates the strong correspondence of responses found in the three subgroups. The differences that can be observed, especially in the graphs, are of a quantitative nature and show differences in degree rather than in kind. Hence the response to FG in poems does not seem to depend on pre-training, as acquired in university course-work in either stylistics or literary analysis. This amounts to saying that exposure to FG affects processes of perception and interpretation regardless of familiarity with the theory of FG itself. Moreover, it also seems to be the case that reader response is independent of familiarity with the text itself. This follows from the fact that in the case of the poem by Cummings more than half of the Ss in the STY-group recognized the poem or its author. Nevertheless, the responses of this subgroup do not differ markedly from those of the two other groups. In view of the strong support found in favour of the independent character of responses to FG as described in this section, such careful sampling of subgroups was not repeated in the design of later experiments.

HYPOTHESIS ELEVEN: ATTITUDES TO POETRY

Prior to the experiment, informants had responded to the Likert scales investigating their attitudes and involvement with respect to poetry. The results of this test, Part A, show a certain scatter over the three subgroups, while at the same time the mean values are in general much lower in the NENG-group than in the other two groups:

Table 4.20
Mean values per statement in the Likert scale

Question	1	2	3	4	5	6	7	8	TOT
STY	4.5	4.6	3.8	3.9	2.8	4.3	4.1	4.5	32.3
ENG	4.6	4.4	4.2	3.8	3.1	4.4	4.3	4.3	33.2
NENG	3.8	2.7	2.8	3.3	2.5	3.7	2.0	3.3	24.0

	Mean	Median	Range
STY	32.3	33	20
ENG	33.2	33	21
NENG	24.0	23.5	28

According to the responses given to the Likert-scales, Ss were then divided into three groups on the basis of their poetry-involvement index, distinguishing groups with a LOW, MIDDLE and HIGH index. The LOW one refers to those subjects whose rating over all eight statements in the Likert scale turned out to be lower than 20 (the maximum being $8 \times 5 = 40$). The MIDDLE group consisted of Ss with ratings between 20 and 30 and the HIGH group of Ss with ratings between 30 and 40. The scatter over the previous subgroups was as follows:

Table 4.21
Distribution of poetry attitudes over subgroups

	STY	ENG	NENG
Low	0	1	7
Middle	4	0	8
High	12	13	7

As can be seen, the greatest scatter is to be found in the NENG-group, which was the most heterogeneous one in terms of university training, while the STY- and ENG-subgroups tend to cluster around the upper end of the scale. To make use of this classification, the data for all tests were retabulated and re-arranged according to these three categories: LOW, MIDDLE and HIGH ratings of poetry involvement.

The major question to be investigated is whether any relationship can be established between Ss' responses and their belonging to one of these three groups. This is examined by a X^2-test of association. The results for Parts B, C and E (nominal data) are listed in Table 4.22. Of the fifteen tests carried out, only two are significant below the set level of $p < .05$. This is the case for the Dickinson poem in both Part C and E. All other results clearly show the absence of any relationship between the vertical axis (subgroups on the basis of poetry involvement) and the horizontal axis (responses to either FG or BG). In other words, apart from these two cases, no evidence can be found (at least not with statistical probabilities) that allow us to make any strong generalizations for a connection between Ss' performance in the test and their own attitudes toward poetry. Whether the two tests that did turn out significantly, are due to chance or to other factors, remains difficult to determine. In general, however, it is not possible to conclude in favour of the opposite hypothesis that a strong correlation between poetry involvement and type of response exists.

Table 4.22
Poetry Involvement: X^2 in subgroups: Low, Middle and High Index

	Part B		Part C		Part E	
	X^2	p	X^2	p	X^2	p
Cummings	.65	.70/.80	3.58	.10/.20	1.44	.30/.50
Dickinson	.41	.80/.90	20.48	.001	12.21	.001/.01
Roethke	.26	.80/.90	1.54	.30/.50	.15	.90/.95
Thomas	1.19	.50/.70	3.95	.10/.20	1.46	.30/.50
TOTAL	1.26	.50/.70	4.46	.10/.20	.38	.80/.90

The second question which should be investigated at this point is whether the responses of LOW, MIDDLE and HIGH groups also conform to the predictions. The nominal data are analysed first.

Table 4.23

Attitude Subgroups as related to Predictions: Binomial and χ^2-tests

PART	STATIS-TICAL TEST	GROUP	Cummings	Dickinson	Roethke	Thomas
	B	LOW	.00003	.0446	.1131	.50
	I					
C	N	MIDDLE	.00003	.0023	.1539	.0132
	O					
	M					
	I	HIGH	.00003	.00007	.00003	.00003
	A					
	L					
		LOW	.00003	.00003	.0068	.2514
E		MIDDLE	.00003	.0838	.00011	.0045
		HIGH	.00003	.00003	.00003	.00003
C	χ^2	LOW	.001	.01/.02	.05/.10	.20/.30
		MIDDLE	.001	.001/01	.05/.10	.001
		HIGH	.001	.001	.001	.001
E	χ^2	LOW	.001	.001	.001	.05/.10
		MIDDLE	.001	.001/.01	.001	.001
		HIGH	.001	.001	.001	.001

It is evident from Table 4.23 that a high proportion of the analyses yield significant results: 39 out of 48 tests have associated p-values below .05, or 81% of all analyses carried out. In these cases subgroup results significantly corresponded to the predictions made. With respect to the insignificant results, a serious methodological reservation should be made. One may notice that they all occur in the L and M groups: 6 in the former and 3 in the latter. But these are the groups that contained fewest Ss: only 8 in the L-group and 12 in the M-group. Such numbers are in fact too small to serve as a basis for generalizations, and any statistical analysis of such small samples is unreliable. The fact that twice as many insignificant results are found in the smallest group (i.e. the L-group, containing 8 informants) adds further strength to this interpretation of the insignificant results. To put the predictions to a more serious test, the scores for groups L and M were conflated and then analysed again for those cases that had yielded insignificant values before. Notice that this is quite a legitimate technique. In some instances of X^2 application it is even advisable; see, for instance, Siegel (1956: 46). All insignificant cases of the previous tests do become significant when this shortcoming of small samples is remedied.

Finally, the ordinal data of the experiment were re-analysed in a similar way. The average ranks obtained for each of the groups, i.e. those with LOW, MIDDLE and HIGH poetry involvement were matched to the predicted ranks with the help of the Spearman rank correlation test. The results of this analysis are to be found below:

Table 4.24
Attitude subgroups as related to predictions: Spearman rank test

r_s	L	M	H	TOT
Cummings	.65	.91	.90	.90
Dickinson	.80	.81	.97	.90
Roethke	.73	.43	.80	.78
Thomas	.98	.83	.91	.90

p	L	M	H	TOT
Cummings	.01/.05	.01	.01	.01
Dickinson	.01	.01	.01	.01
Roethke	.01/.05	< .05	.01	.01
Thomas	.01	.01	.01	.01

As can be seen, correlations between observed and predicted ranks are significant in 15 out of a total of 16 cases. Thus there seems to be good evidence in favour of rejecting the null-hypothesis, and accepting the alternative hypothesis: Ss basically rank order phrases with the help of the same criteria as the experimenter did, i.e. the criterion of FG. One case does not offer support for our claims; neither the theory itself nor the examination of test-results can at present account for it. With the kind of data that have been gathered, any conclusions as to such causes would remain highly speculative. However, this one case can hardly lead one to conclusions in the opposite direction, i.e. accepting an association between poetry involvement and reader response to FG.

So what has been learnt from the regrouping of the data? The conclusion may be formulated in a straightforward way: if Ss are grouped according to an index of their subjective attitudes to poetry, the basic conclusions arrived at in previous sections, establishing a strong link between FG and reader response, are not altered in any significant way. This result, though negative, turns out to be yet another forceful argument in favour of a high generality for the hypotheses derived from the theory of foregrounding.

CONCLUSIONS

From the analysis and discussion of the empirical data some general conclusions may be drawn. Of the four initial variables postulated, three could be accepted as confirming the theoretical model under investigation. Those were the parameters of strikingness, importance, and discussion value. Memorability had to be rejected as a parameter, since its results did not bear out the predictions. As the other parameters correlated well with each other, it is more likely that memorability as a test instrument was inappropriate. The view of memory processes that had been taken in developing this test almost certainly proved to be too naive. Most probably other factors that have a direct influence on recall interfered with the processes set in motion by the FG in the text. It was therefore concluded that Part B should be rejected as a test instrument, but that it was difficult to draw any clear conclusions from these negative results in so far as they bear on the theory of FG. For the three other variables, the evidence found in favour of the theoretical model was very compelling. Only in a few cases did the empirical data conflict with the hypotheses and in some of these cases this may have been caused by an insufficiently large sample. It should be emphasized that for the total sample of readers participating in the experiment, all statistical analyses yielded highly significant results, hence strongly supporting the hypotheses concerned.

Furthermore it was found that inter-subject consensus was high in all cases. Similarly, reader response did not seem to depend on familiarity with the theory of FG, nor on prior literary training or attitudes held towards poetry in general. All these results were corroborated by the variety in the text sample, while there seemed to be some rough indication of a growing consensus among Ss after repeated exposure to the same text. Finally, with respect to the cohesion of FG and its contribution to the interpretation of the text as a whole, the data contain indications of two different hierarchies operating in poetic texts: that of FG and that of thematic structure.

Although in general the two may work intimately together, the present results contain some hints that in particular cases effects of thematic structure may override instances of FG. In those cases the latter may still stand out as most striking, but for the building of an interpretation their importance will be of a lower order.

Chapter Five

FURTHER REFINEMENTS: DESIGN OF INDUCTIVE PROCEDURES

INTRODUCTION

The previous part of this study tried to establish whether any validity could be found for the theoretical claims made by the theory of foregrounding. Although generally the data provided support in favour of the theoretical model, the exact nature of Ss' responses to foregrounding configurations was not yet well enough accounted for. Thus, while Ss seemed to respond differently to FG and to BG, it was difficult, on the basis of the tests involved, to make any guesses as to the precise qualitative difference between these responses. The three initial variables that had been accepted, i.e. strikingness, importance and discussion value, had opened up some general perspective of the quality of reader response. We can say that stretches of foregrounding in a text are generally perceived by readers as more striking, more important, and more worthy of discussion, than corresponding background passages of the same text. However, these three qualities had been deduced from the theoretical model; it was thought relevant to supplement these qualities with inductively collected data which might highlight, on an empirical basis, the properties of the response to FG. The approach followed was thus inductive in nature, and consequently differs from the methodology of the previous part of this study. There the approach could be labelled deductive, since the various parameters were deduced from the theoretical model, and specific hypotheses and predictions were derived from it. The tests and their subsequent analyses provided reasonably clear answers to the question whether or not the predictions were borne out by the data. In investigating the characteristics of reader response to FG, methods in which data are collected in a systematic way but without any precise predictions concerning the outcome, were to be used. This did not imply that <u>any</u> kind of data would fit the bill. The experiments set up here are still geared toward those aspects of the process which one suspects will be relevant to the questions under consideration. In this sense the collection of empirical data <u>does</u> contain predictions, i.e. the experimenter's expectations of where interesting material is to be found. But the nature of such expectations is much weaker than that of predictions formulated in earlier chapters; hence any conclusions arrived at will have to be treated with caution. Care is especially necessary when framing generalizations beyond the scope of the test situations themselves.

Three different areas of research were selected for this investigation. Two of these are concerned with the Ss' responses to FG configurations, while one examines the interrelationship between responses found in earlier experiments, and textual structure. The latter was tested through a multiple regression analysis, the former two by means of a multiple choice test and a test using Osgood's semantic differential. Each of these will be discussed in turn.

THE REGRESSION ANALYSIS

The predictions concerning previous experiments had been arrived at after detailed stylistic analyses had been carried out in successive stages, the results of which were then superimposed on one another. First the level of phonology and graphology in one poem was scanned for FG devices, then the level of grammar, and finally lexis and semantics. For each of these levels an enquiry was made into the presence of four different FG devices: parallelism, and deviation (statistical, determinate and internal). However, there was no indication at that time as to what contribution to the overall effect of FG was made by the four different devices, or which of the three levels would have the most impact when FG devices were located on it. Some rough indication of differences in contributing to the effect of FG was embodied in the scoring system, based on the assumption that the level of semantics would play a more dominant role over the level of grammar, which in turn would provide a more powerful contribution than the level of phonology (see Chapter 3).

In order to investigate this matter further, a regression analysis may be used in the following way: the body of data collected in previous research may be matched to the theoretical model; an examination as to which elements of the model are the best candidates for influencing the response of the reader may then be carried out. This amounts to finding the best correspondence between the IV (the theoretical model) and the DV (the data collected in previous tests). The outcome of such a regression analysis allows one to deduce which of the theoretical variables had the strongest impact in helping to determine the informants' responses.

Represented visually:

The theoretical variables consisted of all observed cases of FG devices, arranged per verse-line and per poem. There were twelve such variables: four devices on three linguistic levels, but, as determinate deviation on the level of phonology was in itself rather rare, the regression analysis worked with eleven theoretical variables.

The empirical data collected in Part C (the underlining test for 'strikingness') were used for this purpose, on the ground that the strikingness parameter follows most directly from the theoretical literature. The data consisted, it will be remembered, of underlined words. Their frequencies were cast into a matrix combining the observed variables (i.e. the number of words underlined, grouped per verse-line and per poem) on the one hand with the theoretical variables on the other hand. The latter were arranged on the X-axis, while the former were set out along the Y-axis in the following way:

	Y	X_1	X_2	X_3	X_4	...	X_{11}
Line 1:	23	2	5	1			6
Line 2:	3	2	0	1			0
Etc.							

In this example informants had underlined a total of 23 words in the first line of the (first) poem, and for this line the stylistic analysis had located two cases of the X_1-device, (e.g. of phonological parallelism), five cases of the X_2-device, (e.g. statistical deviation on the phonological level), and so forth. This matrix is fed into a computer program[1] which calculates the probability of association between any one X-variable and the observed Y-variable, on the ground that Y could be viewed as a function of X, the basic equation of a multiple regression analysis being of the following kind:

$$Y = f (X_1, X_2, X_3, ...)$$

The computer program gives as output the 'best fit' between X- and Y-variables in the form of an equation in which the coefficients for the X-variables highlight their relative importance. A high coefficient for such a variable indicates a high significance of that particular theoretical variable. From a comparison of all coefficients, conclusions may then be drawn as to which variables may be used as best predictors of the experimental results, and which therefore should be given extra weight in the theoretical model.

As will be clear from the example given above, the theoretical variables need to be cast into the matrix in a numerical form. However, the analyses of the poem, as presented in Chapter 3, did not allow a ready quantification of FG features with sufficient objectivity yet. To this end all poems were scanned extensively again, the methods for doing so being made more explicit still. It is not possible to go into all details concerning the various decisions that had to be made at this point. The general reasoning however, needs to be made manifest, as well as the results of this quantification of FG. The latter can be found in Appendix 3, where the various decisions are listed in their numerical form.

Concerning the device of parallelism it was found that the theory had to be seriously constrained. As Culler (1975) and Werth (1976) had shown, parallelism is inherent in linguistic structure as such, and Jakobson's unlimited scanning of a poetic text results in a proliferation of FG cases, so that a clear focus is lost. Use was made at this point of the suggestions for setting up such constraints by De Beaugrande (1978: 3-44). Thus the scope of parallelism was limited to short term memory span. Since this breaks down in about ten to twenty seconds - see Keele (1973), as reported by De Beaugrande (1978: 15) - only parallelisms within this time span were taken into account. Reading times were measured to delimit the number of lines for each poem that would fall within the short term memory scope. However, since some factors in the perception of parallelism might override STM limitations, allowance was made for the following cases to be indicated beyond the imposed constraints: line initial patterning and rhyme position, and the recurrence of words or syllables closely linked to the topic of the poem. For the phonological level further restrictions were made. First of all, stressed syllables only were used. Secondly, only the same (and not similar) vowels or diphthongs were entered and only recurring initial and final consonants. Finally, consonant clusters were indicated, regardless of position. The recurring sounds (within the above constraints) were linked by lines, and the number of linkings for each verse-line were counted as an index of the amount of phonological parallelism in that line.

For the level of grammar a chart was represented, depicting a linear grouping of a rather abstract syntactic structure with a minimum of syntactic categories. Only S, V, O, ADV, PP, APPOS,

CONJ, VOC, REL, and QUANT were used in this analysis. Nouns in the plural were rendered N-s. For the poem by Cummings the categories AUX, COMPAR (comparative clause) and LOC (locative) were also employed, in order to make possible the representation of the deviance in the final line and the parallelism between lines 6 and 10. The same system as the one used on the phonological level (i.e. linking parallel structures by means of lines, and using the number of lines as an index of the amount of parallelism) was used for the grammatical level[2].

On the level of <u>lexis and semantics</u> the number of categories was likewise restricted, but the system was slightly adapted: a full line was used for the recurrence of the same lexical item, dotted lines to represent words that were semantically similar, either through being synonyms (such as, for instance 'dolour' and 'sadness' in the poem by Roethke), or through being part of the same lexical or semantic field or of a similar associative set (such as 'pencils', 'boxes', 'pad', 'paperweight', etc. in the same poem). Finally a line broken with dots depicted semantic contrast between lexical items (for instance, between 'wintry' and 'pleasant', and between 'love' and 'reason' in the poem by Cummings).

As to the device of <u>deviation,</u> the following analytical decisions were made. <u>Statistical deviation</u> on the level of phonology was established on the basis of tables displaying the sound inventory of each verse-line in each poem. These inventories of phonemes were closely inspected and any obvious deviation was listed in its numerical form. For instance, the first line of the Cummings poem contains the only instance of a /k/-phoneme. Such a case is quite conspicuous, and consequently it was included as a statistical deviation. Furthermore, extra weight was given to phonemes that occurred in stressed or in word-initial position. The totals for each verse-line were counted and entered into the regression matrix. For the level of grammar and semantics however, it was not possible to find any rigorous method of quantification. Instead individual cases were pointed out and enumerated for each verse-line.

Cases of <u>determinate deviation</u> on the phonological level as produced by the analyses in Chapter 3 were counted and fed into the regression matrix. Concerning the grammatical level observations of syntactic rule violations were tabulated in numerical form. There is no unit here: a structure that deviates from a rule is simply given one value, for instance an S-O-V structure gets one value, but the lexical rule violation of 'yes is a pleasant country' also gets one. Only cases of lexical rule violation and of subcategorization rule violation are counted as cases of syntactically ill-formed strings, while cases of selection restriction violation were considered as semantically ill-formed. The argument here is that instances such as 'the brain is wider than the sky', 'the sadness of pencils', 'the blind man sees best', etc. present the reader with a processing difficulty in terms of their meaning. (Presumably processing the syntax of these utterances would pose the average native speaker with hardly any major difficulties.) It was not easy to find an elegant representation for the semantic level of all instances of determinate deviation. For the sake of clarity, an atomistic approach was adopted: individual cases of deviation were defined in terms of lexical units, so that they would be quantifiable and hence be useable in the regression analysis. For instance, in the first line of the Roethke poem, a deviation is constituted by the co-occurrence of 'sadness' and 'pencils'. Since this selection restriction violation involves two distinct lexical items, it was given a value of 2. Compare however, the neologism 'skysigns' in the poem by Thomas: this deviation consists of one lexical unit only, and consequently was given the value 1.

In general a problem presented itself concerning the possibility of having <u>internal deviation</u> at the very beginning of the poems. In other words, the question arose whether the first lines of a poem may be said to contain cases of internal deviation, when no pattern has been set up yet. In the analyses it was preferred to allow for this possibility, on the ground that retrospectively a reader may detect such cases. Especially since Ss had been asked to read the poems at least twice during the experiment, allowance has to be made for such a possibility, at least in principle. Nevertheless, some cases still remained problematical and sometimes decisions had to be made almost completely intuitively. On the phonological level, matters were relatively straightforward. The sound inventories were inspected: for each phoneme the tables were read horizontally, i.e. along the dimension of the phoneme's frequencies in all lines of the poem. (The phoneme / ə / was never considered a candidate for internal deviation, on the ground that its systematically unstressed position will make it tend to recede into the background of perceptual activity.) Whenever the frequency of a particular phoneme was considerably higher than its surroundings, the decision was made to view it as a case of internal deviation. To quote some examples: in the Cummings poem the phoneme /iː/ occurs for the very first time in line 9, and then twice in the same line. Similarly, line 12 contains two diphthongs that occur only once in the whole text: /eɪ/ and /ɛə/; as such they were judged to be internally deviant. Note that such instances may occur in words that are intimately linked to the thematic structure of the poem, and this might give special prominence to their significance. In the examples just quoted this is indeed the case. However, in this stage of the analysis such considerations were left out as much as possible. Instead a kind of blind scoring of the phoneme distribution was aimed at, in order to ensure a maximum of objectivity. On the level of grammar, individual cases of internal deviation could not be quantified in any systematic way. Instead observations of individual cases were enumerated. On the level of semantics, the quantification was again carried out in terms of lexical units, as has already been pointed out for the determinate deviations.

All enumerations concerning the different FG devices on the three linguistic levels are included in Appendix 3. The results of the regression analysis will be discussed in the following chapter. No specific predictions are made in advance with respect to the outcome of the analysis: the exercise is geared at acquiring additional information rather than confirmation.

EVALUATIVE RESPONSES TO LITERATURE

Previous experiments could be said to examine reader reactions that depended directly on the way in which FG features in a text were perceived by readers. A number of salient characteristics attributed to this activity of cognition (such as strikingness, importance, discussion value, etc.) were found to be related to textual properties describable in terms of foregrounding devices. However, since theoretical articles on foregrounding recognize the possibility of a link between foregrounding and artistic quality, it was judged imperative to investigate readers' evaluation of foregrounding as well. Although it is not always possible to disentangle aspects of perception and evaluation (see, for instance, O'Hare 1976: 451) it is necessary to investigate both separately, especially since the main dimensions of perception need not be the most salient ones in the act of evaluation. Note that one should also distinguish between preference or evaluation of readers on the one hand and general artistic quality on the other. The latter is difficult enough to define, and in any case may be influenced by various cultural, social and historical factors. As such however, artistic quality is dependent on judgements of individual (and groups of) readers. Therefore a study of evaluative responses of readers will provide interesting (and until now missing) information on the nature of literary value judgements. Two experiments were set up in order to investigate this area: the multiple choice test investigated the measure of preference readers attach to foregrounding configurations. The second (set of) experiments used the semantic differential as a tool for collecting data which bear on the issue of evaluative responses to foregrounding.

The semantic differential

As a first corrective to earlier experiments it was decided to collect data through the elicitation of value statements by informants. In this domain methods of social psychology became highly relevant.

One obvious tool to be used for the present purposes was the semantic differential technique, as developed by Osgood et al. (1957). One of the main reasons for using the semantic differential in this part of the research was that issues of validity and reliability of the instrument have been studied extensively; Heise (1969: 406) speaks of more than a thousand books and articles dealing with this method. At the same time, it allows for a high flexibility in its application. In most cases, the design is aimed at extracting the basic factors that underlie informants' reactions, or at comparing their reactions to different stimuli, the characteristics of which are known to the experimenter. In other words, the semantic differential may be used to establish any difference in, response to either foreground or background configurations of a text. For further discussion of this method, see also Snider and Osgood (1969); on methodological implications in using it, see Heise (1969). It is not possible here to go into all the details concerned with the use of the semantic differential. It should be emphasized though that the instrument has been employed technically, i.e. without subscribing to the Osgoodian paradigm of semantic space, and that therefore the method was adapted to the needs of the experiment. This is not to be considered a misuse of the tool, as may be clear from Osgood's own statement (1957: 76): 'it is a very general way of getting at a certain type of information, a highly generalizable technique of measurement which must be adapted to the requirement of each research problem to which it is applied. There are no standard concepts and no standard scales'.

Notice also that, despite its name, the method does not really measure the 'semantics' of a concept. Instead it probes what may be called associative potential. This in itself is a strong argument in favour of its use, since literature, and especially poetry, has more to it than the mere denotation of words or sentences it is made up of. In any case the present investigation was aimed particularly at these connotative forces of poetry and their resulting evaluative responses in readers. Lindauer (1974: 178) has warned against the risks involved in overdependence on the semantic differential technique, especially if it is used merely as a descriptive tool, at the expense of probing the effects and consequences of literary texts. This danger was avoided by designing two different experiments, the second one of which exactly meets the requirements outlined by Lindauer. These were labelled Part G and Part H respectively. In the former, responses to FG lines were compared to those given to BG lines. In Part H specific cases of FG in poems had been removed artificially, and replaced by lines which were as similar to the original as was possible, but which did not contain a high degree of FG. The sample of informants was subdivided into two halves of approximately the same size, and each of these rated the qualities of either original or of altered lines on the scales.

In Part G informants were presented with three different poems which they were asked to read at least twice: Cummings, Roethke, and (since this poem had been underused so far) Rossetti. Informants were the same as the ones who had participated in Part F. Ss were asked to rate six different verse-lines from each of the poems on five adjectival scales, each containing seven points with a neutral point in the middle. In the first place, two adjective scales reflecting evaluative associations were selected: valuable/worthless and exciting/dull. The former is doubtlessly the clearest of both measures. Snider and Osgood (1969: 506) report high loadings, i.e. .79, for the scale on their first factor, which is the Evaluative one. In another place (1969: 611) they report an even higher loading of this scale, i.e. .91, on the Evaluative factor. The exciting/dull scale loads high, (.40) on the third factor (Activity), but is also related to the pair interesting/boring, which in Berlyne's (1974) research is associated partly with Activity and partly with Evaluative factors. Carroll (1960: 286) also found very high loadings for this scale on his first factor, labelled 'General Stylistic Evaluation'. For these reasons exciting/dull was considered mainly as an Evaluative scale, although it also has associations with the Activity factor. The scale significant/insignificant is similar in this respect. It was selected as an alternative to 'meaningfulness' and 'importance'. The latter two qualities are similarly linked to the Evaluative factor (.41 and .38) and to the factor of Oriented Activity (.25 and .31): see Snider and Osgood (1969: 611). Carroll (1960: 286) similarly found confirmation of this double aspect of the scale in his literary research. The pair surprising/expected was included because it refers to aspects of novelty and is thus clearly associated with foregrounding. Especially since this aspect of the notion of foregrounding may be conceived of in informational theoretical terms such as 'surprise', it was thought favourable to include a pair surprising/expected along with the other scales. Moreover, the pair might represent an interesting correlation with the 'strikingness' variable that was investigated in earlier experiments of the present study.

The fifth pair, poetic/prosaic is not reported in the literature to date. It has been introduced to test the intuition that stretches of foregrounding in a text might attract higher ratings of poeticality than background parts. Martindale (1973) has advanced a similar claim: he reports on an experiment in which informants had to rank order samples of various approximations to English[3]. His findings indicate that ratings of poeticality drop off sharply above third order approximations, while ratings of grammaticality drop off sharply below fourth order approximations. He concludes that 'poeticality has to do with statements which are of a distinctly lower degree of grammaticality than that which characterizes prose' (1973: 23). While this seems to provide interesting confirmation of the effects of deviance as a foregrounding device, it is difficult to see how effects of poeticality due to parallelism relate to Martindale's findings. It is also dangerous to generalize his results, as they are based on eight informants only. In the present study a larger sample of informants was used, and poeticality judgements were geared at real poems. In these, passages that are prominent because of parallelism as well as those that are in the foreground because of deviance, occur.

In the design of the present experiment, care had been taken to confront Ss with three lines from the FG and three lines from the BG of each of the three poems used. An instruction page clarified how the scoring was to be carried out, and Ss could keep this sheet in front of them during the test. The order of presentation of the three poems was randomized to counterbalance any effects due to fatigue. The main object in this test was to find out whether average group ratings for the FG-lines would be different from those given to BG-lines. No specific predictions could possibly be made as to the outcome of the experiments at the time, but in general it was expected that FG-lines might display a tendency to attract higher positive ratings on these five scales than BG-lines.

In a later experiment session, Part H, a second test with the use of the semantic differential, was run. This time however, original lines in the poems (by Dickinson, Roethke, Rossetti and Thomas) had been altered in such a way that specific foregrounding devices were removed from them. Hence a new line, now belonging to the background, which in all other respects was kept as close as possible to the original one, replaced the originally foregrounded line. Without Ss being aware of it, they had been divided into two subgroups, in such a way that approximately half of them received poems with original (FG) lines kept intact, while the other half received doctored versions of the poems, in which particular FG features had been removed from some lines and had been replaced by similar wordings but without any conspicuous foregrounding devices. For a rationale of this technique, see Berlyne (1974: 18). After introduction and presentation of the poem, Ss were asked to rate the lines on a number of semantic differential scales. This time thirteen scales were used, in order to investigate a wider range of properties of foregrounding, but also in order to allow us to carry out factor analyses on the data: see Berlyne (1974: 16) and Heise (1969: 419-421). The selection of the scales was carried out in a somewhat different way than for Part G. First of all, the poetic/prosaic dimension was retained. Apart from this scale, the 'dictionary' of adjective pairs presented in Chapter Two of Osgood (1957: 53-61) was investigated for useful pairs. Among these, the scales that had been used in Part G were included. The selection of evaluative scales was completed by the pair interesting/boring. Usually the choice of the scales is done on intuitive grounds, i.e. pairs are included of which the experimenter suspects that they will reveal interesting characteristics. At the same time, however, it is important to mask the experimenter's aims by throwing in some adjectives that are more difficult to see through for the informants, but that nevertheless bear a relationship to the other pairs. It is common practice to select about three adjectives from each of the main factors discovered by Osgood, so as to avoid measuring one dimension only. In the present design it was decided that the Potency scales strong/weak, deep/shallow and large/small would sufficiently mask the objectives of the experiment. To a lesser degree, the same may also hold for the three Activity scales that had been selected: exciting/dull, active/passive, and complex/simple. Finally, the idea of investigating aspects of novelty, as was started by the surprising/expected pair in Part G, was retained. To this end the scales new/old and usual/unusual were added. The total number of thirteen scales corresponds to other designs generally employed, which use between ten and fifteen pairs. So as not to impose too heavy demands on the informants in terms of scoring time, only four lines per poem were presented.

Alterations to the poems had been invented by the experimenter. It should be pointed out, however, that it proved notoriously hard to do this in a completely consistent way, as removing one foregrounding feature often resulted in the smuggling in of another. To quote one example only, in the first line of the poem by Dickinson, 'The Brain is wider than the Sky', the word 'wider' was replaced by 'greater', in order to take out the chiming effect of the /aɪ/ in 'wider' and 'sky'. However, by doing this, one has, without intending it, introduced another parallelism instead, i.e. the chiming that can now be observed between the /eɪ/ of 'brain' and 'great'. In general considerable effort was taken to control these factors as much as possible. The altered versions of the poems are included in Appendix 1, and the alterations have been underlined.

The results of both Part G and of Part H were investigated by comparing the group data for all lines (see Appendix 2G and 2H). In the former experiment, a comparison was made between responses to the FG lines and those to the BG. In Part H the average responses to original (FG) lines were compared to responses given to the corresponding altered (and hence supposedly BG) lines.

The multiple choice test

At an early stage in the development of this experiment it was conjectured that readers might show a marked preference for foregrounding configurations in the reading of poetry. This was derived from the functional nature of foregrounding, as described in various theoretical works; see, for instance, Mukařovský (1964a: 47), Leech (1969: 56), Jakobson (1960: 358-359). If foregrounding offers the reader a rewarding experience in terms of a fresh and unexpected perception of the world, or in terms of the fulfilment of an aesthetic need for patterning, then readers might be expected to show a high degree of preference for FG over BG items in a poetic text. To this end special versions of the poems were prepared. In these, a number of original words had been deleted, while for each deletion Ss were offered five alternative lexical items to choose from. They were then asked to select the one they preferred. Care was taken in all cases to mix randomly the original item among the four distractors. The first task then consisted in finding good alternatives for the original words in the poem. For the sake of objectivity, it was important to guard against any bias which might be introduced. Consequently, it was assumed that the danger of a self-fulfilling prophecy might be too great if the experimenter himself provided the alternative versions. Instead real readers, who were not aware of the experimenter's aims, were asked to provide the distractors. Cloze versions of all poems were prepared in the following way. Every fifth word was deleted in every poem, starting with the first word in the poem. In this version the first, sixth, eleventh, etc. word was replaced by a dash of standard length. A second version was then prepared in which every second, seventh, twelfth, etc. word was deleted, and so on, until five different cloze versions of all poems had been prepared. These were multiplied and sent to a number of other Universities and Colleges of Higher

Education who were prepared to cooperate with the project[4]. All versions which were returned were then tabulated and compared. Only the poems by Cummings, Roethke, Thomas and Wordsworth yielded full versions with distractors for all deleted slots. Hence these four poems were used in the experiment. In order not to make the task too demanding for informants, it was decided to delete five words only in each poem. Secondly, in order to gain some insight into the possible differences between Ss' preferences for either FG or BG, both categories were proportionally represented in the number of deletions in each poem. According to the theory, it should not matter too much which lexical item fills a BG slot, as long as it is still BG. However, in the case of FG, the discrimination of Ss between the original item and BG distractors should be marked. Thus the pull of distractors would have to be stronger in cases of BG deletions than in cases of FG deletions. Thirdly, only lexical words were selected, with the sole exception of the closed list item 'yes' in the first line of the Cummings poem.

All data obtained through the cloze versions were scanned and interesting locations, both in terms of foregrounding and in terms of available distractors, were indicated. Finally, a selection of five alternatives for each deletion was made. This was done mostly on the basis of the possibility of rank-ordering the distractors in terms of increasing degree of foregrounding. These decisions were tested intersubjectively with M.H. Short, then supervising the study, and 'multiple choice'-versions of the poems were then prepared. Concerning the formulation of the specific task for Ss, it was decided to compose two subgroups, each of which was given a different task. For half of the Ss the task consisted in selecting the item from the five distractors which they would insert at that particular place if they were themselves the poet drafting a final manuscript. The other half of the group was asked to do the same, while considering themselves to be a scholar faced with five different manuscripts of the same poem, each differing only slightly in a number of words from the others. They were then asked which of the distractors would, according to their intuitions, be the word originally employed by the poet. The procedure for collection of data was organized in two rounds: a large number was collected through questionnaires that were sent through the internal mail to students of Lancaster University. It was also decided to run a small test of this kind in an experimental situation. This was labelled Part I, while the collection through questionnaires was termed Part J. Samples of the test forms of these procedures have been inclued in Appendix 1.

NOTES

1. I am grateful to M. Aitken and to B. Francis of the Centre for Applied Statistics at the University of Lancaster for computer assistance and guidance in this analysis.

2. It should be pointed out that charts depicting grammatical PAR were scanned first for the longest stratches of PAR. (For instance, in the Dickinson poem, lines 1 and 5 were first linked by a line indicating a completely PAR structure between the syntax of these two lines.) The remainder of the text was then inspected for shorter stretches of PAR, and so on, until the whole text had been exhausted in this way. In general no allowance was made for 'overlapping' of shorter with longer stretches of PAR.

3. These were approximations to English as developed by Miller and Selfridge (1950). The sets of strings of varying degree of approximation to English were printed on index cards and randomized. Ss were then asked to rank these in order of increasing 'poeticality'.

4. I should like to express thanks to the following people for their help in collecting these data: D. Burton (Birmingham University), R. Fowler (East Anglia University), L.M. O'Toole (Essex University), M. Stubbs (Nottingham University), M. Wiles (West Midlands College of Higher Education, Walsall) and S. Woolford (Cambridge University).

Chapter Six

FOREGROUNDING IN TEXT AND READER RESPONSE

INTRODUCTION

The data collected in these experiments have been tabulated in Appendix 2. Generally these are in the form of nominal data (number of preferences for alternatives in the multiple choice test) or of ordinal data (average group responses on semantic differential scales). The outcome of the regression analysis will require separate treatment. It should be remembered that data were collected to gain further insight into the processes that are at work when readers are confronted with foregrounding in a text. As such this part is more explorative in nature. Consequently the tentative nature of the results obtained should be emphasized.

THE ANALYSIS OF THE 'MULTIPLE CHOICE' TEST

For the data collected in this part of the study, see Appendix 2 I and Appendix 2 J. The questionnaire allowed us to collect considerably more data than the experiment: a total of 105 forms was returned. The sample of informants was composed of two subgroups which we will refer to as 'poets' and 'scholars': those who considered it their task to 'compose' the poem in the same way the poet had done, while the other group tried to guess what items had been in the original as if they were scholars faced with different manuscripts all deviating slightly from one another. However, through an administrative mistake, a large proportion of the informants did not return the initial page containing the instructions, so that for 60% of the questionnaires it was not possible to retrieve to which subgroups they belonged. These responses are listed in the Appendix as 'not indicated'.

Since care had been taken to provide distractors for both FG and BG items in the text, it is possible to compare Ss' choices for both categories, and to enter them into a contingency table of the following kind:

Table 6.1. Preference prediction

	FG lines	BG lines
Original items	a	b
Distractors	c	d

where c < a > b   (a is greater than both $\underline{b}$ and $\underline{c}$)
      c < d > b   (d is greater than both $\underline{b}$ and $\underline{c}$)

If one speculates that there be a connection between FG and readers' preference, then the number of times they preferred the original items must be higher than the number of times they selected distractors[1]. As can be seen from Appendix 2J, the prediction is borne out in questionnaire results in the following manner: preference for distractors is always highest in the BG lines, hence confirming the predicted relationship $\underline{c < d > b}$. Concerning the relationship between FG lines and original items, however, things are more complicated. In the poem by Thomas, original items are preferred more often in FG than in BG lines, thereby affirming the prediction $\underline{a > b}$, while $\underline{a > c}$ is negated. For the poem by Roethke even the relationship $\underline{a > b}$ is not observed. Hence the generality of predicted preference for FG items cannot be supported. What does become clear from the data, however, is that original FG items are preferred with a frequency that is well above chance levels. For instance, in the poem by Roethke, the originals in the FG lines (1), (8), (13) were selected by 27, 28 and 63 Ss, while the expected value (for n = 104) lies at 20.8. The x^2-test reveals that this distribution is not random (p < .001). The same holds for the poem by Thomas. There, moreover, the positive relationship between FG/BG-lines and original/manipulated items is confirmed at a high level of significance (x^2 = 67,55, p < .001).

Concerning the data of Part I, it may be observed that the prediction b < a > c is borne out in the Wordsworth poem, while b < d > c is confirmed in the Cummings poem, at least if one concentrates on the total results of each text. As for the subgroups ('poet', 'scholar') it should be pointed out that the number of informants is too low to allow for any clear conclusion.

The relationship between FG and reader preference may also be investigated with the help of x^2 , indicating whether informants' selections of alternatives are related to the nature of the items under consideration, i.e. their being original or manipulated.

Table 6.2 lists the obtained x^2 and their associated p-values for Part I (Experiment), while Table 6.3 does the same for Part J (Questionnaire). As can be seen from the former, none of the x^2-tests for the experimental data are significant below the critical level of 5%. Confirmation of the hypothesis that it is the low number of informants in the sample (i.e. 10 and 14 in each subgroup) that causes the insignificance, may be derived from the fact that in the Cummings poem a rank ordering of p-values in order of significance matches exactly a ranking in terms of the number of participants in the test.

Table 6.2. x^2 tests of PART I data

	Cummings		Wordsworth	
	x^2	p	x^2	p
Poet	1.02	.30	.82	.30/.50
Scholar	1.14	.20/.30	.00	1.00
Total	2.15	.10/.20	.04	.80/.90

Thus the smallest group (i.e. 'poet', with 10 Ss) has the lowest x^2 value, and the largest group (i.e. 'total', with 24 Ss) the highest, with the middle group ('scholar': 14 Ss) having a x^2 value situated between the previous ones. In the Wordsworth poem, however, this is not confirmed. There all differences (if any) in reaction are negligable and must be attributed to chance rather than to stimulus quality.

Study of <u>Table 6.3</u> reveals that all x^2-values for the Thomas poem are highly significant, while those of the Roethke poem yield one significant[2] and one highly significant value. Two subgroups, i.e. 'scholar' and 'not indicated' do not yield statistically significant results.

Table 6.3. x^2 tests of Part J data

	Roethke		Thomas	
	χ^2	P	χ^2	P
Poet	15.2	.001	14.0	.001
Scholar	.15	.70	39.8	.001
Not Indicated	.36	.50/.70	93.4	.001
Total	3.58	.05/.10	145.3	.001

It may therefore be said that the questionnaire data confirm the general hypothesis much stronger than data collected in Part I. Nevertheless, in view of two clearly insignificant results, strong care should be taken in supporting any generalization concerning the relationship between foregrounding and preference. Rather such a relation manifests itself as <u>a tendency</u>.

So far, however, the analyses have not taken qualitative differences between distractors into account. For instance, the first line of the Cummings poem was provided with the following alternatives, of which (b) was the original:

———— is a pleasant country
     a. Mine
     b. Yes
     c. Norway
     d. Love
     e. This

As will be clear from the example, at least one of the distractors, i.e. (d), should also be viewed as an instance of foregrounding, because it violated a selection restriction rule. (It is less foregrounded, though, than the original 'yes', which also violates a lexical rule.) Inspection of the data reveals that this distractor (d) had the highest preference among subjects! Together with (b), the only other foregrounded item among the alternatives, they attracted 96% of all preferences by informants. It should further be emphasized that neither of the two items that would have made the line into a BG one (i.e. 'Norway' and 'This') were selected. This must be interpreted as an indication that the readers preferred foregrounded items in this line, even though they did not always select the original poetic choice. Notice that the opposite holds too. For instance, the third line of the same poem was presented in the following fashion, in which again (b) is the original wording:

(my—————————)
     a. dear
     b. lovely
     c. word
     d. cold
     e. god

In this list, items (a), (b) and (e) are definitely BG, but (c) and (d) - because they deviate from the surrounding context - must be considered as (slight) instances of foregrounding. Thus in this line, which belongs to the BG of the text, readers could have introduced some measure of FG if they had wished. The remarkable thing is that they did not. Items (c) and (d) were chosen by 1 informant only, against 23 for the remaining (BG) items. Here again one observes how readers strongly adhere to the original pattern of the text, without however necessarily having recourse to the original wording of the poem. The difficulty here (partly caused by the fact that the alternatives had been provided by other readers through the cloze-procedure) is how to differentiate the measure of foregrounding between alternatives such as (a), (b) and (e), which all seem to be of relatively equal status in a BG/FG-hierarchy. It is similarly difficult to distinguish items such as (c) and (d) in terms of a foregrounding hierarchy. The demarcation line between BG and FG, on the other hand, does seem to be relatively easy to determine.

In order to further investigate readers' preferences vis-à-vis foregrounded items in the text, a quantitative analysis of the following kind was undertaken. All alternatives provided were divided in two classes (BG and FG) and grouped according to the verse-lines in which they occurred. (Note that the position held by verse-lines within the BG/FG dichotomy had been unambiguously established already in Chapter 3.) When alternatives have thus been entered into contingency tables a X^2-test may reveal to what extent an association exists between Ss' preference for an alternative on the one hand, and its status within the FG/BG-dichotomy on the other. Retabulation of the data from this perspective shows the following distribution:

Table 6.4. Distribution of FG preference

		Distractors	
		FG	BG
Cummings: lines	FG	26	22
	BG	7	41
Wordsworth: lines	FG	50	22
	BG	4	44

As may be seen in Table 6.4, both predictions, b < a > c and b < d > c are confirmed. Moreover, X^2-values for each poem are highly significant, i.e. well below p < .001. The conclusion from this investigation may be clear. Although at first sight no clear preference for FG items seems to be given by Ss, a more detailed analysis does reveal a positive relationship to exist between them. There is a strong tendency to select FG items in FG lines, especially if the nature of the alternatives with respect to their being foregrounded is taken into account. That these are not always identical to the original FG words indicates that the tendency does not depend on the exact originals, but manifests itself as a more general preference for foregrounded configurations as such.

When we examine the data on the <u>Wordsworth</u> poem, we find that in all subgroups, the two most FG-ed items, i.e. 'mind' (line 1) and 'divine' (line 8) are preferred by informants in an unambiguous way: 71% and 84% respectively. The other FG line (7) does not produce such a straightforward picture. It should be pointed out that, although the original item ('Stranger') was not selected, the two other vocatives among the distractors, ('Brother' and 'Friend'), which produce a line with almost equal FG, are selected more than any other items: together they constitute 55% of all choices. The one case that does not fit our assumptions is line 4, where the BG item 'chase' is preferred by 60% of the Ss. Note however, that the slot needs a transitive verb, and that three of the distractor verbs do not meet this specification. Of the remaining verbs, 'turn' and 'chase', only the latter produces the strong rhyme.

It should be clear by now that the connection between FG and reader preference is not an absolute one, but manifests itself as a tendency. The question then becomes how strong this tendency is. The X^2-tests have already given some indication, but we now need to look at the results in more detail. In the data of Part I, two subgroups and one total were examined, while Part J provided data of three subgroups. Every case in which the Ss of these groups showed a marked preference for distractors in the BG lines and for originals in FG lines was counted as a confirmation of the tendency. As a refutation the cases where Ss preferred distractors in FG lines and originals in BG lines were counted. In this way the following quantification of the previous discussion may be arrived at:

		Confirmation	Refutation
Part I	Cummings	10	5
	Wordsworth	8	7
Part J	Roethke	10	5
	Thomas	10	5

It should be mentioned that of the 'refutation' cases six do not deviate very much: these are the three subgroups preferring other vocatives to 'Stranger' in the seventh line of the Wordsworth poem, and the three subgroups that preferred another FG item (i.e. 'love') instead of the original 'yes' in the first line of the Cummings poem. Consequently, the general pattern that emerges from the results is that confirmation of the relationship between FG and reader preference is found at least twice as often as cases that go against such a relationship. Note that the general ratio of confirmed to refuted cases remains fairly stable over the four poems: approximately 66% of all cases confirm the theoretical claim, while 33% falsify it. It should be stressed that such a ratio is far too weak to accept a general model predicting a necessary link between FG and personal preference. On the other hand, considering the multitude of factors influencing readers' decision making processes in such a situation, it is remarkable that the tendency in favour of a relationship displays itself in such a strong form, and with such an apparent stability over different text stimuli. It could therefore be the case that in this area of personal preference, considerable differences between individuals may exist, and that consequently any theoretical claims can only be made as weak predictions, i.e. in the form of a general tendency. This does not mean that the theoretical model must therefore be declared valueless, as an analogy with election poles might demonstrate. If candidate A is consistently preferred by twice as many informants as candidate B, one could predict with a high safety margin that A would win an election between them. In the same way the tendency of readers to prefer FG items above BG ones is quite marked, and the odds seem to be strongly and consistently in its favour. In order to widen the scope of the confirmation of such tendency and to narrow down the cases refuting it, it might be necessary to take other factors concerning the individual's background (such as, for instance, age, sex, education, socio-economic status, personality traits) into account.

THE ANALYSIS OF THE SEMANTIC DIFFERENTIAL EXPERIMENTS

Both Part G and Part H make use of the semantic differential instrument. Since both yield a rather large body of data, and since they try to capture different aspects of FG, they will be treated separately. In Part G, six lines were used from three different poems; these were rated on five scales by a minimum of 26 Ss. Together, this produces a total of 2340 measurements. Similarly, Part H made use of four different lines from four different poems, which were rated by 24 Ss on 13 scales, thus yielding almost 10,000 different statements concerning Ss' judgements of the qualities of the lines.[3]

The results of part G

In the experiment, the directionality of the scales was randomized, in order to counterbalance any possible effect due to standardized ordering. In the tabulations in Appendix 2G, care has been taken to convert all data into the same direction. Hence the values for the different lines can be interpreted in terms of real positions on a bipolar scale. As numerical values, medians were used throughout. This was done because the median, as a measure of central tendency, is less affected by extreme scores.

In the first place, data were inspected in order to find out which lines (FG or BG) attract the most positive statements, i.e. which lines are judged as most poetic, valuable, significant, exciting, or surprising. The tables contain the median value of the total group of informants for each of the six lines employed on each of the five adjective pairs that were used to elicit Ss' statements.

The picture is clearest in the poem by Cummings. The FG lines (9 and 12) are consistently to the positive end of the scale, except on the final one. The remaining FG line (1) does not fit the expectations: on the first scale it scores low, while on the middle three scales it occupies a middle position. Only on the expected/surprising scale does it score highest. On the other hand, lines 9 and 12 occupy a middle position on this scale. On the whole then, the BG lines (3, 7 and 8) evoked less positive responses, although there are some instances where this is not the case.

For the poem by Roethke, the picture is less clear, in the sense that many more cases may be observed that conflict with the assumption that a relationship might exist between FG and qualitative statements by readers. First of all, the BG lines (4, 5 and 10) score higher than one FG line (1) towards the positive end of the scale poetic/prosaic. On the significant/insignificant scale, little difference between FG and BG lines can be observed, but FG lines are more towards the positive end. On the valuable/worthless scale two conflicting cases should be noted: line 4 (BG) scores higher than line 13 (FG) and line 10 (BG) in turn does better than line 1 (FG). A similar tendency may be observed for exciting/dull: line 10 (BG) does better than line 13 (FG), and the BG line 4 scores higher than the FG lines 1 and 8. Finally, the expected/surprising scale shows low values for the FG lines 8 and 13, but a very high value for the FG line 1. Although this presents a much more diffuse picture, it should be pointed out that the lowest positions are occupied by BG lines (5 and 10) on three out of the five scales, while the highest positions are taken by FG lines (13, 1 and 8) in four out of five cases.

For the Rossetti poem one notices a strong clustering of the lines, but in general the direction of the oppositions between FG lines (1, 9 and 10) and BG lines (3, 6 and 12) corresponds to the predictions. On the significant/ insignificant dimension, hardly any difference between lines can be observed. On the poetic/prosaic scale, line 6, although of a

BG nature, takes a higher position than the FG lines 9 and 10. The FG line 10 also seems to answer least to the claim that FG should evoke a stronger positive reaction in the reader: it scores lower than the BG line 3 on three different scales: valuable, exciting and surprising. Here again, however, the general picture confirms the expectations: the lowest values are occupied by BG lines (6 and 12) throughout, while the highest positions are always taken up by FG lines (1 and 9).

In sum then, data show group medians not to be distributed randomly: they run parallel in most cases, with a noticeable tendency for the FG lines to be a more powerful source of positive response than BG passages from the poem. As such this finding confirms the conclusions from the multiple choice test: the relationship between FG and aesthetic quality is not an absolute one, but rather one of tendency. This tendency, although not verifiable in all cases, is nevertheless too strong to go unnoticed. In order to test the significance of this tendency, a binomial test was carried out. First of all, (for each of the scales) the number of FG lines was multiplied by the number of BG lines scoring lower on that scale. Conversely, the number of BG lines was multiplied by the number of FG lines scoring lower. The obtained frequencies were then entered into the tables for the binomial test. Table 6.5 summarizes these results:

Table 6.5
Distribution of positive response: bionomial test

	z	p≤
Cummings	- 3.21	.0007
Roethke	- 1.06	.14
Rossetti	- 2.80	.003

As can be seen, the distribution yields highly significant results for the Cummings and Rossetti poems; for Roethke the p-value is not significant.

However, there exists a second method by which to put the hypothesis concerning a possible relationship between FG and qualitative statements of readers to the test: the median test. The median value for the total sample is first calculated; then the data are scanned for the number of observations above and below this combined median, which are then cast into a 2 x 2 contingency table and a X^2-value is calculated. If the test yields significant probabilities, it indicates that the medians of FG and BG categories differ sufficiently to warrant the conclusion that a relationship between FG and qualitative judgement must exist. The results of the median test are summarized in the following table:

Table 6.6
Relation foregrounding/positive ratings (Median Test)

Scale	Cummings	Roethke	Rossetti
Poetic	3.82 *⁴	.008	9.17 **
Significant	11.66 **	4.88 *	.006
Valuable	4.92 *	6.76 **	.003 ?
Surprising	.93	.005	3.07 ?
Exciting	20.04 **	2.24	2.86 ?

* significant below .05
** significant below .01
? significant below .10

On the basis of chance one could expect 5% of these tests to turn out significantly, i.e., almost 1 in 15. However, inspection of the results reveals that 8 out of 15, i.e., 53% are significant below the conventional region of rejection. These high p-values occur for four different scales, so they are spread out over the different dimensions. It is perhaps significant too, that the Cummings poem contains the lowest p-values; this might tie up with intuitions concerning the effects of FG in overtly modernist poetry. In general then, the number of significant results of the median test does not allow a straightforward falsification of the hypothesis concerning a connection between FG and judgements of quality. However, as before, the connection is not of a necessary nature.

Further conclusions to be drawn from the experiment concern the fact that significant results found in the application of statistical techniques are scattered over the three poems and over the five different scales used. Hence the tendency is not linked or limited to any one particular text or to specific scales. Since in previous experiments it has been demonstrated that readers agreed to a large extent over what was FG (in terms of parameters such as 'strikingness', 'importance' and 'discussion value') it would follow that these observed agreements are hard to split into separate constructs such as poeticality, significance, and the like. It rather seems to be the case that they all work together in some way or other. The effects of FG must therefore be understood as the result of a complex interaction, and FG itself may be described as a <u>holistic</u> concept, in the sense that its effects may be due to a variety of factors, and that these interact. Hence it is not possible to point to one attribute of a poetic text as being the cause of the processes typified as FG. Consequently, when asking Ss for a general and overall response, fairly good correlations with the predictions are found. When such overall response is split up between different variables, the data match predictions much less well.

How complex the interaction underlying the holistic nature of FG is, can be observed when one studies the group medians obtained on the scale expected/surprising. On the basis of the literature on FG, one would expect that FG lines would evoke more 'surprise' answers than BG lines. However, close inspection reveals that all three poems provide instances where this is not the case. In the Cummings poem, lines 3 and 8 (BG) score higher on this dimension than the FG lines 9 and 12. In Roethke, lines 13 and 8 (FG) are similarly surpassed by the BG lines 4 and 5. In the Rossetti poem, line 10, although FG, is more 'expected' than line 3 (BG). Notice, however, how the first line of every poem consistently scores high on this dimension, except for the Rossetti poem, where it is only surpassed by line 9. It would seem to be the case, then, that the responses to FG for this scale interact with the linearity of the poem's structure: initial lines attract much higher ratings on this scale than succeeding lines, and vice versa, final lines do less well on this dimension: in the data for the Roethke poem, the final line, which, nevertheless, is the most FG-ed in the poem, scores lowest of all on this adjective pair. Also in the Cummings poem, lines 12 and 9, and in Rossetti, lines 10 and 12, all FG, score considerably lower than could have been expected on the basis of their status in the FG hierarchy. But it should be wrong to conclude from this that the primacy principle works in such a simple way. First of all, both the Cummings and Roethke poems provide examples of lines which score low on the 'surprise' pair, and are not end-lines. Furthermore, in the Rossetti poem the initial line is surpassed in this respect by line 9. Instead it is suggested here that the principles of primacy and of FG interact in a complex way. This in itself may throw some doubt on the information-theoretical approach to FG. The fact that FG features must carry high information value, and therefore be felt as more 'surprising', as has been suggested in the literature, cannot always be confirmed by the data. Instead it seems to be only one of several factors that influences the reader's reaction. Making a distinction between 'semantic' and 'aesthetic' information, as Moles (1968: 124) does, does not solve the problem. Moreover, recent criticism of the collative-motivational model - see, for instance, Berlyne (1974) - is aimed precisely at this information-theoretical aspect. In this vein, Konečni and Sargent-Pollock (1976) and Steck and Machotka (1975) showed that aesthetic choice was dependent on other factors besides information-theoretical ones, such as the range of stimuli used and the processing capacity of Ss as depending on the demands of the experimental task. There seems to be no a priori reason why similar factors could not have constrained the predictive power of FG elements in the text. Therefore it is suggested here that the effects of FG configurations do not solely depend on surprise effects as described in information-theoretical terms. Instead a conglomerate of several dimensions seems to be at work simultaneously.

Two final issues concerning Part G should be dealt with. The first one is a tentative explanation of the fact that some FG lines score low on the prosaic/poetic scale. For instance, in the Cummings poem, line

1, although FG, scores lowest of all lines. In the Roethke poem, line 1 similarly scores lowest in terms of poeticality, while line 13, also FG, is highest, together with line 10, which is clearly BG. It is proposed here that the reason why lines attract high positive responses on this dimension may have little to do with their being FG or BG, but rather with the amount of phonological patterning found in them. For instance, line 1 in the Roethke poem contains some assonance, some slight alliterative effects, and a statistically prominent number of /n/ and /s/ phonemes. But compared to the strong effects observable in line 13 these look very bleak. Compare: the strong (i.e. stressed) assonance in 'glazing', 'pale', 'grey', 'faces', the spondees in 'pale hair' and 'grey faces', the stressed alliteration of 'grey' and 'glazing', the echoing effect of 'duplicate' with 'delicate' of the previous line, and the slighter effects of alliteration: 'duplicate'/ 'standard', 'pale'/ 'duplicate'. Together these make the final line much more dense in phonological patterning than any other one in the poem. In a similar way, line 8 shows considerably more phonological PAR than lines 1, 4 and 5, and this corresponds to their median scale values. The data of the Cummings poem also support this view: lines 9 and 12 show more phonological PAR than line 1, but it is more difficult to explain why line 1 is situated lower on the graph than the BG lines 3, 7 and 8, none of which contains conspicuously more phonological patterning than line 1. Hence the tentative nature of the explanation advanced here should be stressed. Further control over this variable may reveal whether the devices of PAR have different effects than those of deviation.

The results of Part H

When the results of both groups are compared (see Appendix 2H) it is clear that removing FG from the poems had in general a quite marked effect: group medians for original and for altered lines differ in most cases. This is an interesting result in itself. One assumption of present-day criticism holds that works of art are unique organic wholes. The metaphor of equilibrium is consequently employed in art evaluation. The opposite is usually associated with tension, and its effects are described rather in negative terms; see also Kreitler & Kreitler (1972: 87). Concerning issues of FG, one may in this respect think of Mukařovský's (1964a: 45; 1964b: 66) notion of the 'indivisibility' of the literary work of art. If this assumption holds, then any change in the structure of a work would upset its balance, thereby destroying its aesthetic effect. Recent work in experimental aesthetics has questioned this assumption. Even when quite drastic alterations in the colour, form or composition of paintings (as presented via slides) were made, Gordon & Gardner (1974) could not find any significant differences in informants' reactions to originals and altered versions. Such findings cannot be corroborated in the research reported here. It is abundantly clear that the changes that had been made in the poems, did evoke a different response. Whether this is due to the specific nature of literature (as opposed to the visual arts) remains hard to say at the moment. The results do seem to provide confirmation, however, for the theoretical notions of indivisibility and uniqueness.

A second striking feature of the results, however, is the fact that the alterations made in the poems are not always judged negatively by informants. In a number of cases the altered line is even preferred to the original one, in the sense that it evoked more, or stronger, positive responses than the original. In this respect we are in a similar position to that of Noll (1966) who found that almost 60% of his Ss preferred a computer generated pattern which was less organized than Mondrian's painting 'Composition with lines' (1917) to the original work by Mondrian.

One case deserves special attention in this respect. Line 10 of the Rossetti poem is rated consistently (on all scales but one) as more positive in its altered form. Close inspection reveals that the line ('My silent heart, lie still and break') is highly repetitive and strongly mirrors the previous line ('Lie still, lie still, my silent heart'). The alteration considerably reduced the amount of PAR in the line: 'The final hope let me forsake'. It seems to be the case then, that a reduction of PAR is welcomed by informants as more rewarding. Perhaps modern readers do not appreciate abundant PAR or repetition in literary texts. This hypothesis receives further support from the following observation.

In general, the original lines are judged as more positive, i.e. in 62% of all cases. This figure is comparable to the 66% of informants preferring original FG items in the 'multiple choice' test. Again we are faced with a tendency rather than with a clear-cut situation. Moreover, the positive responses allocated to original lines are not distributed equally over all poems. Compare, therefore, the following figures:

Table 6.7
Preference for original lines

Dickinson:	17 scales, i.e. 33%
Roethke:	44 scales, i.e. 85%
Rossetti:	21 scales, i.e. 40%
Thomas:	45 scales, i.e. 90%

The two modern poems apparently provoked more positive associations to the original lines than did the two 19th century poems. It should be noted that in the latter, mainly devices of PAR had been removed, while in the former especially deviant configurations had been altered. This seems to provide interesting confirmation of the hypothesis advanced by Leech (1969: 74) that tropes (foregrounding irregularities of content) are 'more powerful in effect' than schemes (foregrounded repetitions of expression). Since this matter is also related to the relative importance of the different descriptive levels (semantics being the typical level of organization of tropes, grammar and phonology being that of schemes), we will return to it in discussing the results of the regression analysis.

An investigation of those differences in response that were statistically significant, confirms this argument. The median test was applied for this purpose. Only 10% of the observed differences, however, turned out to be significant at the level of .05. Notice that, although this number is low, it is still twice as large as could have been expected on the basis of chance alone. It should be emphasized, though, that the samples to which the median test is applied here, are small, thus preventing really firm generalizations.

Again, the significant results are not spread out evenly over the four poems. The Dickinson poem has two, the Rossetti poem three, Roethke six and Thomas eleven. Hence, the poems from which deviation had been removed provided the strongest difference in response: three times as many significant median tests are produced for those poems, as compared to the poems in which the devices removed were predominantly of a parallelistic nature. Notice that in four cases, Ss rated the altered line significantly more positively than the original one. This is the case for lines 3 and 10 of the Rossetti poem (on scales 10 and 2 respectively), line 7 of the Dickinson poem (scale 12) and line 7 of the Thomas poem (scale 11). In each case, except the last one, the altered line contains less parallelism than its original, hence lending support to the explanation suggested before.

Summarizing what has been found so far, we can say that in general, tampering with FG in poetry does lead to a different reader response, albeit not necessarily so. About two-thirds of the original lines (containing stretches of FG) are preferred by our readers over manipulated versions (lacking such FG configurations). Only a small proportion of these differences were significant in a statistical sense. This presumably is related to the rather low number of participants. Of those which were significant, however, the majority was in the direction predicted: higher positive ratings for FG lines. Finally, this tendency was more marked in the two modern poems. Since these were also the poems in which mainly devices of deviance had been manipulated, this may indicate a more favourable attitude of informants toward these devices. Indeed, the complementary tendency could also be observed: removing devices of parallelism had in general a less negative effect on Ss' responses. In some cases this even led to a significantly higher evaluation of the manipulated line.

Since in this chapter the relationship between FG and evaluation is at stake, we need to ask whether the observed differences played a foremost role in Ss' rating activity or were simply a by-product of the task. In other words, did Ss themselves make use of evaluative criteria in responding to the lines? If they did not, then this might invalidate the previous findings. A factor analysis was therefore carried out. This simultaneously allows us to gain more insight into the general stucture of readers' response to poetry. Factor analysis tries to detect any overall correlations in a large body of data. As such it is a technique of ordering the data collected by use of the semantic differential, and consequently of identifying the main principles and classifying them. Child (1970: 2) defines a factor as a cluster of related phenomena: 'when a group of variables has, for some reason, a great deal in common a factor may be said to exist'. The simplest factoring method, i.e. principal component analysis, was selected as most suitable for our design, on the basis of the fact that it does not impose very strong assumptions on the variance found in the data. In other methods, the communality of the variance is estimated on the basis of correlation matrices. In principal component analysis 100% of the common variance is used in the analysis. Nie et al. (1970) advise the researcher to use the PA1 method, i.e. principal components without iterations, as it does not demand a high expertise in factoring methods. As we were most interested in extracting factors, rotation processes that emphasize factor building were selected. The Varimax method was chosen as the most appropriate technique in this respect. Appendix 2H lists the various matrices and factor scores that were obtained for both the original and altered lines. In each case, the factor matrix may be inspected for the highest coefficients. For the original lines, it shows high values for the valuable/worthless scale (.84), for the strong/weak scale (.72), for the interesting/boring scale (.70) and for deep/shallow (.69). Since all of these values are significantly higher than the loadings of other scales, one may conclude that the first major factor is a cluster of these four scales. Since two of these adjective pairs are of an evaluative nature, and two refer to Osgood's Potency factor (strong/weak and deep/shallow) one might label this first factor as the evaluative-potency factor. In a similar vein one may inspect the loadings of the second factor: these are high only on the scales new/old (.90) and unusual/usual (.58). Since both refer to aspects of novelty, one might call this the <u>novelty factor</u>. Again the loadings for the other factors may be scrutinized and interpreted. As the number of factors progresses, their contribution in the overall variance explanation diminishes rapidly. This can be seen in the table containing the latent roots, or the 'eigenvalues' of the different factors. For instance, the eigenvalue of the first factor is roughly five times larger than that of the second factor; from there onwards the eigenvalues drop below one. Usually factors with such low eigenvalues are not taken into account when interpreting the factor analysis. Hence we are left with three factors, the first of which accounts for 48.4% of all variance, the second one for 10.3% and the third one for 7.8% of the total variance. Together they explain 66.5% of all variance found in the data.

In each of the computer plotted graphs below, each time one factor is represented by the horizontal axis, while another factor is plotted on the y-axis. The coordinates of the thirteen scales used in the experiment are a function of their relationship to the factors that have been extracted through the analysis. Thus the first graph clearly shows how the first (horizontal) factor is made up the scales 2, 7, 9 and 12, while the second factor (i.e. on the vertical axis) is composed of the adjective pairs 8 and 10.

Figure 6.1 Principal Component Analysis
Factors I and II

1 = Large   6 = Significant   10 = Unusual
2 = Valuable   7 = Strong   11 = Active
3 = Surprising 8 = New   12 = Deep
4 = Exciting   9 = Interesting   13 = Poetic
5 = Complex

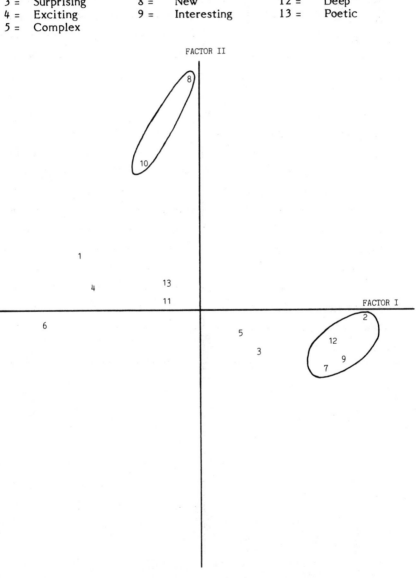

Figure 6.2 Principal Component Analysis
Factors I and III

1 =	Large	8 =	New
2 =	Valuable	9 =	Interesting
3 =	Surprising	10 =	Unusual
4 =	Exciting	11 =	Active
5 =	Complex	12 =	Deep
6 =	Significant	13 =	Poetic
7 =	Strong		

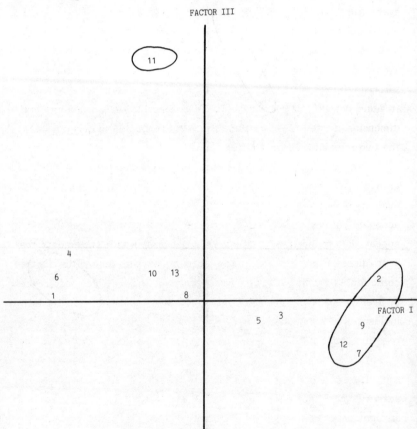

The second graph shows how the first factor contains the same four scales (2, 7, 9, 12) clustered at the right hand side of the x-axis, while the third factor emerges a the top of the y-axis. It consists of one scale only: the active/passive pair. This in part explains why this third factor contributes little to the total variance found.

A similar procedure was followed for the altered lines. Again, three factors are considered on the basis of the eigenvalues, together accounting for 62% of the total variance. However, the factors extracted are slightly different here. The first factor, accounting for 41% of the total variance, consists of the same variables, but the second factor (with 12% of the variance) contains two other scales: surprising/expected and complex/simple. The third factor also differs: it again consists of one scale only: large/small. Thus, while the main dimension (factor 1) is the same as for the responses to original lines, the two remaining factors differ.

The first factor is obviously an evaluative-potency factor in both groups. Thus the major dimension underlying Ss' response is of an evaluative nature: evaluative scales, together with potency scales, account for most of the variance found in the data. It would therefore appear that reader reaction is mainly concerned with statements that bear directly on the value and potency of the text. This further consolidates the validity of earlier analyses: the observed differences in average response to original and altered lines cannot be said to be incidental. On the contrary, they must be ascribed to the fact that reaction to the lines was largely determined by an evaluative attitude.

The second factor is difficult to interpret in the data bearing on the altered lines: scales representing Osgood's factors of novelty, activity and potency all merge into it, thus impeding any straightforward interpretation. This is not the case, however, for the corresponding (second) factor relating to the original lines. There two scales, directly referring to novelty make up the factor. Since aspects of novelty are frequently invoked in theoretical treatments of FG, this must be taken as an indication that the experience of novelty does indeed play an important role in the reading of poetry. In the altered lines, we have apparently, together with the devices of FG, destroyed this element in reader response to the text and this resulted in the evaporation of a clearly defined second factor.

Little can be said about the third factor. It differs for both experimental conditions, and it is composed of one scale only. Moreover, they account for a very low proportion of the variance found in the data, so it is wise not to attach too much importance to it.

THE REGRESSION ANALYSIS

The matrix containing both theoretical and empirical variables needed for the regression analysis is found in Appendix 3. Line numbers 1-12 refer to the Cummings poem, 13-24 to the poem by Emily Dickinson, 25-37 to the Roethke poem, and 38-46 to the Thomas poem. For ease of reference, the symbols used for the theoretical variables are explained below.

Table 6.8
Theoretical variables used in regression analysis

Variable name	FG device	Linguistic level
X_1	Parallelism	
X_2	Statistical Deviation	Phonology
X_3	Internal Deviation	
X_4	Parallelism	
X_5	Statistical Deviation	Grammar
X_6	Determinate Deviation	
X_7	Internal Deviation	
X_8	Parallelism	
X_9	Statistical Deviation	Semantics
X_{10}	Determinate Deviation	
X_{11}	Internal Deviation	

The data for Part C were entered as empirical variables, and the performance of the three subgroups (see Chapter 2) was compared. A first product of the regression analysis is the analysis of the variance found in the data. The results are found in the table below:

Table 6.9 Analysis of variance for all data

Source of variation	Degrees of freedom	Sum of squares	Mean square	Variance ratio
Between groups	2	87.6	43.8	10.6
Subjects within groups	49	202.6	4.1	
Total	51	290.2		
Between lines	45	1758.3	39.1	23.0
Group X line interaction	90	158.0	1.8	1.03
Residual	2186	3721.0	1.7	
Total	2321	5637.5	2.4	
Grand Total	2372	5927.5		

As can be seen from the high variance-ratio value between groups (10.6), real differences exist between the group count means for the three different samples of informants. This means that the average number of underlinings per line differs between the subgoups. The following table summarizes the group means.

Table 6.10
Group means of number of words marked per line

Group	Mean
STY	1.50
ENG	1.35
NENG	1.06

The table shows a steady decrease in average underlinings from the top to the bottom of the table. In other words, the average number of words indicated by Ss as 'striking' decreases with the groups' expertise. Thus, while Chapter 4 did not reveal any significant difference in <u>what</u> Ss belonging to the subgroups underlined, the more experienced Ss are likely to mark considerably <u>more</u> words than less experienced Ss. Moreover, the variance ratio between lines is very large (23.0). In other words, the differences in average number of underlinings per line is quite significant. This reinforces our earlier conclusions that the line-stimuli do not present equal possibilities (except in terms of chance) for the underlining task. We may reinterpret this finding in terms of the experiment by saying that FG lines attract considerably more attention (and hence underlining) than BG lines.

Of greater interest is the small value of the variance ratio for the group-by-line interaction. The overall differences in group means are indicated here as being consistent from line to line; that is, on average, any line of poetry chosen will exhibit essentially the same group differences. This is yet another confirmation of the conclusions arrived at in Chapter 4: differences that can be observed between the groups are not large enough to constitute a significant result. Hence we may conclude that all groups display the same kind of response to FG; any differences between groups are matters of degree, not of fundamentally different ways of reacting to the FG in the lines.

The regression analysis was further employed to find out whether the response of Ss can be predicted by forming some linear combination of the FG variables: and if so, which of the theoretical variables are most important in estimating the response of a subject. Standard multiple regression techniques were used, regressing the mean response for all Ss in a group against subsets of the theoretical variables for each line. The appropriate regression equations are given in the table below. For each subgroup the predicted value of the response ($\hat{R}$) is given by the appropriate linear combination of theoretical variables. Different such FG variables are necessary for each of the three groups. The standard errors of the regression coefficients are given in parentheses.

Table 6.11 Multiple regression equations for each group

Group	Regression equations
STY	$\hat{R} = -0.164 + 0.059\ X_3 + 0.206\ X_8$
	$\quad\ \ (0.124)\quad (0.019)\quad\ \ (0.008)$
ENG	$\hat{R} = \ \ 0.451 + 0.051\ X_2 + 0.258\ X_{10}$
	$\quad\ \ (0.094)\quad (0.008)\quad\ \ (0.041)$
NENG	$\hat{R} = -0.102 + 0.084\ X_1 + 0.092\ X_8$
	$\quad\ \ (0.114)\quad (0.015)\quad\ \ (0.017)$

The equations may be interpreted in the following way. For the STY-group, the regression equation shows that the mean number of effective words (i.e. FG words) increases by 0.059 with each unit increase in X_3, and increases by .206 with each unit increase in X_8. Correspondingly, for the ENG-group, the increases are .051 for X_2 and .258 for X_{10}. Similarly the NENG-group shows an increase by .084 for X_1 and by .092 for X_8.

In each group, two theoretical variables suffice to explain a fairly large proportion of variation in the data: 56% (STY), 54% (ENG) and 43% (NENG) respectively. But the variables themselves are not constant over subgroups. Inspection of Table 6.8 reveals that they are the following ones:

Table 6.12
Most important variables per subgroup

	Phonology	Semantics
STY	Internal Deviation	Parallelism
ENG	Statistical Deviation	Determinate Deviation
NENG	Parallelism	Parallelism

It can be seen that the regression analysis isolated variables from only two levels: phonology and semantics. Not one variable from grammar seemed to play a prominent role in the strikingness of the text. This goes against our assumption of the relative increase in importance from phonology to grammar to semantics. It seems, at least according to our data, that the formal level of linear organization plays but a marginal role in perceiving the strikingness of a text. A caveat should be made here, because the syntactic analysis took into account only general issues of surface grammar. Instances of selection restriction violation, for instance, were assigned to the level of semantics.

The relative weight of both phonology and semantics may be tested by comparing the coefficients found in the regression equations. These are summarized below.

Table 6.13
Regression coefficients for linguistic levels

	Phonology	Semantics
STY	.06	.21
ENG	.05	.26
NENG	.08	.09

It is clear from the table that the coefficients for the level of semantics are higher in all cases. Notice furthermore, that for the STY- and ENG-groups, the difference is quite marked, while the untrained Ss of the NENG-group make a less sharp distinction. In general then, the conclusion may be warranted that the level of meaning is of considerably more importance than the level of sound. Discounting the relative unimportance of FG devices on the grammatical level, our assumption about the semantic level exerting a greater influence in the reading process, finds strong confirmation here.

A second striking pattern to be observed in the results of the regression analysis is the preference of the untrained informants (NENG-subgroup) for devices of PAR in their response, while literature students (the ENG-group) are hardly geared at PAR at all. Instead, these readers make use of the devices of deviation in their reading response. This correlates with the fact that DEV may introduce tension in the text, while PAR heightens redundancy. Hence trained readers may display higher tolerance thresholds for tension (DEV) than untrained readers; compare Kreitler & Kreitler (1972: 16-22).

Finally, it is clear that little agreement is found between subgroups. This must be taken as an indication that readers' background, in terms of familiarity with theoretical notions and with professional training, do differ in the way they respond to textual structure. It is in the employment of these different textual devices that major differences between subgroups can be identified. The fact that this nevertheless led to significant correlations in inter-group performance, may be interpreted as evidence for the notion of nexus, as introduced in Chapter 1. It can be seen that the existence of such a multi-layered structure of FG, operating simultaneously on different linguistic levels, allows readers to select different FG devices in their response to the text, and yet largely agree as to what must be considered as striking in the text. Without the convergence of different devices into a nexus, the correlations between groups could hardly have occurred.

NOTES

1. Since the number of FG and BG lines were not equal, a correction of the frequencies had to be made. When three FG lines and two BG lines had been selected, the frequencies of the latter were multiplied by the factor 3 and those of the former by the factor 2, to allow both groups equal chances.

2. Notice that the X^2 value of the subgroup 'total' only fails marginally to be significant. The required value for the test to be significant at the 5% level is 3.84. The value of 3.58 in our results was judged to be critically close to the level of significance and consequently it was accepted as supporting the hypothesis.

3. Note that, although this seems a high number at first sight, it is by no means exceptional. Most designs aimed at carrying out a factor analysis of the data obtained through a semantic differential test, work with a minimum of 10,000 measurements. Because factor analysis was only a side issue of our design, our slightly lower number was not thought to be hazardous to the general research aim.

4. These results are not significant at the 5% level, strictly speaking. However, it was thought that they approach it close enough to warrant their inclusion in the significant results. The reader may compare:

    $p = .05$ for $\chi^2 = 3.84$

    $p = .10$ for $\chi^2 = 2.71$.

Chapter Seven

GENERAL CONCLUSIONS AND OUTLOOK

Any empirical investigation must, to avoid sterility, be fed back into the theoretical framework from which it originated. Such is the purpose of the present chapter. Let us start therefore by summarizing in general terms what has been gained so far. The literature concerning the concept of FG has been reviewed and discussed in Chapter 1. On the basis of this it was possible to outline a general standard form of the theory. The dominant mode in using these theoretical notions in stylistic practice, has been that of <u>textual</u> analysis. Since the theory also makes claims with regard to <u>effects</u> of FG on readers, it is remarkable that no empirical research had actually studied such presumed effects. Note that this is in no way a new problem; Hymes (1960: 130) stated it already a quarter of a century ago:

> a limitation which, as far as I know, all stylistic approaches share is the making of untested assumptions about the psychology of poet or audience. Many of these assumptions are reasonable and intuitively correct to the student or practicioner of verbal art. But we do not in fact know that the use of a sound in one part of poem has any effect on a reader ... Rather, we analyze the poem, construct an interpretation, and postulate (or instruct) the reader's response.

This deficiency provided the rationale for the decision to empirically probe this neglected aspect of the theory. A series of experiments, the design and administration of which have been described in Chapters 2 and 5, revealed a number of issues bearing on the psychological dimension of the theory. Foregrounding, as defined in operational terms such as 'strikingness', 'importance' and 'discussion value', was found to be strongly related to the stylistic devices of FG, as described by a close textual analysis of the poems (see Chapter 3) used as test materials. Compared with other parts of the texts, the FG passages were a strong predictor of reader reaction. This held for all texts, and for all subject-groups, regardless of familiarity with the theory, prior literary training or attitudes towards poetry. There were also strong indications that inter-subject agreement was considerably higher than would be expected at face value. Foregrounding devices further seemed to constrain text-interpretations. In general, then, such findings would seem to validate the psychological claims advanced by the theory of foregrounding. However, it was also found that other textual principles of organization, such as thematic structure, might interfere with, or even override the effects of foregrounding.

Furthermore, as was demonstrated in Chapter 6, a relationship between FG and reader preference may be accepted, but only in the form of a tendency. The same holds for evaluative reactions to FG passages in a text, whether in comparison to BG lines from the same poem, or to manipulated lines in which FG devices had been removed. Generally, this tendency is in favour of the FG items in two-thirds of all cases. It also appears that falsification in this respect was hard to determine on any singular dependent variable, but usually manifests itself on different scales for different test-stimuli used. That Ss did respond in a predominantly evaluative mode, however, was confirmed by the factor analysis, which simultaneously revealed novelty to be an important dimension in readers' reactions to FG. Moreover, more powerful positive associations were produced by the device of deviation (in comparison to those evoked by the device of parallelism). Differences do exist between subgroups in their use of various FG devices while responding to the texts, while for all groups devices located on the descriptive levels of phonology and semantics explain a high proportion of the variance in the data. Finally, devices on the semantic level proved (as had been assumed by way of a working-hypothesis in Chapter 2) to be of greater impact than those found on other levels of description.

So, in general these findings confirm the predictions derived from the theory of FG. Moreover, the confirmation seems to be independent of personality variables, texts, or experimental constructs and procedures. Could we, therefore decide in favour of the (purportedly universalistic) claims concerning the literary reading process, as developed within the framework of the theory? The temptation to rapidly jump to this conclusion may, in the light of the evidence accumulated, be high. Yet the jump may be risky. What is at stake here is that a set of quantitative data, collected by means of a partly stereotyped procedure, is matched against predictions derived from a theoretical model bearing on a particular human action, i.e. the reading of literature. Although experiments of the kind employed here present highly valuable tools to explore the claims made by such theories, one should at the same time be careful in interpreting their results. A naive (reductionist, or neo-positivist) stand in such matters may easily blind one into unwarranted beliefs in having discovered the 'laws' of literary experience. It would seem wiser, instead, to screen the quantitative data critically, and to subject them to a (complementary) qualitative analysis.

One reason to be modest concerning the results obtained here lies in the limitations of the study. For one thing, the text-corpus used is not as extensive as one would wish. Secondly, only few informant variables have been controlled. Age, for instance, was not; nor was socio-economic class. Principally, it is possible that taking such variables into account might produce a different picture than the one painted in the present study. Further experimentation would be desirable here, although one faces the methodological problem of how to control <u>all</u> variables, a problem inherent in all quantitative methods of research in the social sciences.

Or could it be that Ss had merely provided socially desirable answers? That Ss' goal-expectancies influence test-results, is known from the literature: see, for instance, Duchastel & Merrill (1973), Faw & Waller (1976). However, Ss' complying in this respect would entail their having access to the experimenter's intent. Clearly this was not the case. Up to a certain degree, this intent was masked. Thus, under the high demand and the apparently subjective nature of the task involved, it seems unlikely that participants could have been able to provide socially desirable answers.

Another, perhaps more serious objection against treating our data at face-value only, could be formulated with reference to communal value and knowledge systems bearing on literature, as shared by both experimenter and Ss. High correlations between predictions and responses would not, in this view, be evidence of the effect of FG devices, but merely mirror socially learned responses to literature. Schooling, for instance, would suffice to explain the patterns of correspondence between stylistic analyses and readers' reactions. Most individuals, having spent a considerable number of years in school, have internalized specific ways of responding to literary texts. Stylistic analyses, so the argument runs, simply pays tribute to these underlying value and knowledge systems concerning literature.

Since this argument questions the legitimacy and reliability of stylistic analysis, let us consider it carefully. One way by which to strengthen the objection still further would be to point to similarities between the experimental situation and a classroom situation. The data in this study have indeed been mediated through a highly particular social situation, i.e. that of the experiment, which although resembling individual reading activity in one's spare time, also differs from it in a non-trivial way.

In fact, the experimental situation resembled less that of a private reading situation than that of a reading classroom at school. Let us consider some characteristics of the experimental situation which are compatible with the structure of institutionalized discourse found in classrooms.

(a)   The experiment took place in a room belonging to an educational institution, i.e. a university.

(b)   Participants were seated individually at tables, and were asked not to talk with each other during the time the experiment took place.

(c)   Subjects were provided with pens and paper; the task involved reading and writing.

(d)   The experimenter was standing in front of the group of participants, and was in charge of the situation.

(e)   The power distribution between experimenter and participants was asymmetrical; all activities were experimenter-initiated. All participant-initiated activity involved demands for elucidation. As such, the experimenter wielded symbolic power over participants.

(f)   Subjects were not aware of the ultimate goals of the task, or of the experimenter's (hidden) aims.

The projection by subjects of these characteristics on to a classroom situation may further have been enhanced by one particular part of the instructions given. In the procedure where subjects were asked to indicate which text-parts they personally found worth discussing, the instruction was completed by the clause 'pretending you are an English teacher working with 16-year old youngsters'. In this way, participants may have been provided with a direct hint at similarities between both experiment and classroom situation. The fact that they themselves were students, may have further contributed to a smooth acceptance of the resemblances.

Yet, in spite of all these arguments, the experimental results obtained cannot be dismissed by a facile reference to educational practice. One rational argument against it is the limited amount of elements in the school curriculum that directly point to issues of foregrounding. Ss' exposure to the ideas proposed by the theory of foregrounding within the context of the school is simply too low to allow such an explanation, at least in any extreme way. We do know that they almost certainly had not been confronted with the idea of foregrounding in any direct or explicit way. Most of their teachers were unaware of the theoretical work of Russian Formalism or Prague Structuralism. Nor were they familiar with more recent attempts in stylistics to embed these earlier notions into a more linguistic framework. It may be the case, of course, that ideas on literature, more indirectly linked to the theory of foregrounding may have been present implicitly in the approach to poetry at school. If this be the case however, then one would, given the British educational system (in which some orientation toward specific disciplines may set in at a rather early stage), expect to find at least some systematic variation in subjects' reactions, correlating with the amount of this implicit teaching received. In other words, one would expect there to be, on the basis of considerable differences in exposure time to presumed implicit teaching of foregrounding, corresponding differences between the reactions of subjects in our sample. No indication in this direction has been detectable in the data. Intergroup differences revealed by the regression analysis bear on quite different matters altogether, and in any case did not show that Ss with longer exposure to implicit teaching of FG at school matched predictions any better than did the other groups. On the contrary, the ENG-group, by its dominant preference for the devices of deviance, provides a counter-indication. Hence it is perhaps safer to consider this objection against our results with great caution.

Thus if any influence of educational practice is to work on Ss' responses, it must have been formed in early socialization. Secondary socialization, as in our societies typically taking place in school, may or may not enhance these primary socialization practices, but in general it cannot by itself account for the nature of our Ss' responses. In primary socialization, however, practices that do come close to the ones described by the theory of foregrounding may be observed, a fact to which we shall return instantly. This would mean, then, that the influence of early socialization must be very powerful: it must be able to reach over and beyond the long and sometimes dominant influence of the school. The trouble, however, is that little is known about literary practices in the early socialization stage. In contrast to language development, which is well-documented, few descriptive studies on literary development in the early years of childhood have been carried out. Hence we are at a loss when it comes to the question as to which forms of usage of literary phenomena occur in infant-schools, families, children's play-groups, etc. The evidence that does exist, moreover, has usually been collected with different purposes in mind (e.g. the study of linguistic or cognitive development), and is as a rule scattered over a number of different disciplines, such as linguistics, ethnography, psychology, anthropology, folklore.

One fact, however, and an important one is the high frequency with which FG devices do occur in most of the typical sub-genres of children's (often oral) literature, such as: counting out rhymes, nursery rhymes, songs, fairy-tales. There can be little doubt as to the material presence of a high number of FG devices in the great majority of these texts. Alongside this, one may observe the high willingness of children to join in such activities from an early age onwards. Apparently the texts present special attractions to children. They learn them by heart spontaneously and continuously try to explore (and indeed make up) new ones. One may nowadays also notice young children's interest in (TV-)advertising, noted for its use of FG devices by Mukařovský. Finally, one may also examine the intense delight experienced by young children when engaging in such pre-literary activities.

These observations raise an important issue. The readiness to engage in the activities described and the apparent satisfaction derived from them being so frequent and so wide-spread at such an early age in childhood suggest these activities have some (important) function. Remember in this respect that FG, as described in Chapter 1, is characterized by its functional nature too. What is at stake here, is the anthropological status of foregrounding in particular, and of literature in general. Its relative significance in early child-rearing practice leaves little doubt as to its importance. Determining the exact functional nature of that importance proves to be much harder though, and falls outside the scope of the present study. If it is to be answered, it will demand careful and detailed empirical study. The present situation, in which hardly any studies with respect to early literary development are available, is highly unsatisfactory. I wish to suggest that issues of FG do lend themselves particularly well to such a purpose.

The previous paragraphs have considered the question as to how individuals come to learn about foregrounding. This issue, important as it is, nevertheless stands unresolved. The data obtained in the present study, however, were provided by adults. As the analyses revealed, the textual properties as described by the theory of FG were responded to by readers in a generally predictable way. This brings us to the question of the linguistic contribution to the literary text and its production/reception. That literature is dependent for its very existence on the linguistic medium, is hardly a controversial issue nowadays. The question has rather become: how?

The devices of foregrounding, like most stylistic phenomena, bear on actual linguistic realization. This means that (certainly in a narrow interpretation of the theory of FG) its devices are to be situated on the level of linguistic form. In the case of parallelism formal elements or features are repeated, while deviance displays forms that deviate from others that would more normally have been used. But such linguistic realizations do not occur in a social void. They are, first and foremost, selected by the author of the text as a means of acting linguistically (and hence socially). In other words, foregrounding devices are not merely instances of linguistic ornamentation, but are embedded in the totality of the linguistic and social activity author and reader engage in. Foregrounding devices, in this view, are linguistic means which author and reader have at their disposal for realizing particular aims. These aims, however personal they may be, are necessarily embedded in the social structure and cultural conventions in which author and reader find themselves. This entails that an author may only realize his artistic aims successfully if readers are at least in part able to recognize and appreciate these aims, and if they are willing to participate in a communicative interaction with the author by means of the text.

The question again is: how? And to what extent is it dependent on FG? Everyday communication, with its face-to-face interaction has all the evident characteristics which make it succeed in a usually non-problematic way. Written (non-literary) communication often takes its anchorage points in the institution from which it emanates. So, for instance, the language used in newspapers and magazines depends for its communicative functioning on common and widespread linguistic practice in the institution of the press. Similarly technical or scientific journals contain highly specific forms of language use, typical for these institutions. But how is one to imagine the process of literary communication?

It is here that pragmatics may be of help. In order to execute specific communal plans, answering to corresponding social needs and aims, individuals will often make use of language, by way of linking several speech acts together. Such strings of speech acts usually acquire a pattern-like quality, according to the purpose to which they are used. These patterns may be grounded in everyday interaction, as is the case with such patterns as greeting, talking about the weather, asking questions, or telling jokes. They may also be grounded in social institutions of a culture, as, for instance, giving evidence in court, lecturing, or delivering a sermon. The way in which language is put to use in these instances shows it to be pre-structured to a certain degree. In other words, the particular contribution made by a participant is constrained and shaped by the speech action pattern in which it occurs. Participants are bound by such constraints. In fact, knowledge of a pattern has to be integrated into an individual's total knowledge system as a prerequisite for participating appropriately in the pattern. Such knowledge as a rule results from experiences with the patterns concerned, and may vary greatly in complexity, depending on the kind of pattern. Within the field of pragmatics, some advances have been made with regard to rather simple speech action patterns, such as the ones mentioned before. When it comes to more complex patterns however, the problems involved in an analysis are still immense.

Literature, from this vantage point, is similarly a patterned form of interaction between participants, having its own internal structural qualities and prerequisites. Needless to say, it is a pattern of very high complexity, and one which is not yet very well understood. One of the difficulties in this respect is the seemingly endless capacity of literature to absorb various forms of language use which are common in everyday life or in institutional situations. The language of literature, one could say, is an intricate network of rudiments of various more simple patterns (often connected to everyday and to institutional forms of communication), which have been amalgamated and then as an amalgam undergone a long series of transformations in the course of history. For instance, reading literature may contain rudiments of listening to everyday stories, or of what has been termed by Ehlich & Rehbein (1980) homiletical discourse, i.e. a form of social discourse which does not so much (as is the case with institutional discourse) strive toward the realization of specific aims, but rather to the pleasure and the delight experienced by its participants. At the same time, the speech action pattern called 'literature' may contain rudiments of institutional patterns, such as, for instance, religious rituals, patriotic propaganda or vernacular didactics of religion. At this moment the precise connections between literature and these different kinds of speech action patterns are as yet not well understood. For this reason it is not possible to accurately describe in full detail the nature of the speech action patterns that come into being when literature is being read. However, in order for the author and reader to successfully engage in literary communication, an appeal to some common ground is an absolute prerequisite. I propose to consider this common ground as general cultural knowledge in the form of being familiar with specialized speech action patterns.

Virtually the only road which is open to author and reader to build and exploit such a common ground, is by means of the text itself. The author may appeal to the reader's cultural knowledge by means of specific textual devices, while the reader is bound to reconstruct such an appeal, taking his cues from the linguistic means employed by the author in order to make his appeal. Hence a reader has to hypothesize, on the basis of specific characteristics in the linguistic utterances of the text, what kind of speech action pattern is aimed at by the author and which he may subsequently acknowledge and join in. Only on the basis of such a mutual recognition and cooperation may the act of literary communication be successful. In the case of written literature, which often manifests a great distance between reader 'and writer (who is often no longer alive at the time the reader confronts the text) such cues are particularly imperative.

Turning back now to the nature of FG, the following suggestion is made: foregrounding devices are first and foremost linguistic means allowing readers to identify (and subsequently activate knowledge and motivation concerning) the kind of communicative activities associated with the reading of literature. Hence parallelism and deviance may play a crucial role in allowing participants to identify the speech action pattern as a literary one. If this hypothesis holds, then it allows us to more fully understand and explain the nature of the experimental results reported earlier. Ultimately, such an analysis will lead to the conclusion that subjects have indicated text locations of which the linguistic structure displayed overt markings of the literary speech action pattern. Foregrounding then, is not a category indicating 'essentials' of literariness in an absolute or material sense: it is not so much the text in itself that 'contains' elements of literariness, but rather that specific devices, i.e. those that (perhaps among others) have been described by the theory of foregrounding act as cues to the reader in the process of literary communication. This description of the communicative process in which author and reader must cooperate at least in part, and which may be brought about by marking the text against the shared pattern-knowledge possessed by them, ties in with the empirical results collected in the experiments. The conclusion which emerges is that literary texts tendentially possess a certain degree of markedness, in terms of foregrounding devices, in order to allow readers to reconstruct (and join in) a literary pattern of communication.

This still leaves open the question of how to explain the occurrence of FG in other than literary texts. This is a problem which faced Formalists and Structuralists alike, and which has hardly received a satisfactory solution. Without being able to sort out all the intricacies involved, two suggestions are made. Firstly, certain speech action patterns displaying FG, such as, for instance, nursery rhymes, children's songs, jokes, or riddles, are simply of a pre-literary kind, having their roots in oral cultural practice and tradition. The difficulty here is obviously of a terminological nature: by what standards is one to say that particular texts are 'literary'? Are oral texts to be considered as 'literature'? To an ethnographer they would; literary theorists, however, prefer to concentrate on written texts and to expel oral texts from their field of study. Secondly, FG devices may be used in other than literary texts, such as advertising or election slogans, to acquire some degree of 'literariness'. Producers of such texts may decide to make use of FG devices because of beneficial side-effects they may engender. These effects may run parallel to those invoked by the reading of literature, thereby obliterating the frontier between literary and non-literary texts. This shows the opposition to be misleading. If it is framed in terms of a dichotomy, it can easily be disproved. If it is framed in terms of a continuum, a much more realistic description may be arrived at. At the same time, it should not be forgotten that FG does not equally occur in all types of texts, and that even where it does show up in obviously non-literary texts, it often lacks the cohesion and density it usually reveals in literary texts.

It may be interesting to notice that indirect support for the conclusions formulated in previous paragraphs may be drawn from a different set of experimental data, as reported on by Van Peer (1983). There the strength of associations found between the occurrence of foregrouding devices in a text and readers' preference for such text locations could be ordered along a chronological dimension representing the age of the poem:

Table 7.1
Percentage of negative effects of manipulation

	% of cases
Cummings	85
Thomas	54
Dickinson	44

As Table 7.1. shows, tampering with foregrounding devices in an older text, i.e. the 19th Century poem by Emily Dickinson was judged negatively by readers in only about half the number of cases as with the highly modern writer, E.E. Cummings, and with the results of the poem by Dylan Thomas situated in between.

Although this may seem odd at face value, what has been said before about foregrounding, as marking the literary nature of the speech action pattern involved, may throw some light on this phenomenon. It may be the case that in the history of western literature, past centuries have witnessed (due to a number of technological and sociological factors) a break-down of the traditional bonds between artists and art-consumers. (One may think of this evolution in terms of a growing private reading practice, against a decreasing public encounter with literature; examples may be provided by the rapid increase of mass literacy and mass production and distribution of written literature in the past 150 years, or the gradual disappearance of court culture and court-poets, salons, literary coffee shops, reading circles, etc.) The net effect of this evolution may have been that generally authors must gradually have recourse to more (and more powerful) devices of foregrounding. By doing so, readers may have gradually become accustomed to such powerful devices. In this way, devices employed by authors of a previous era may be experienced by present-day readers as more mild cases, the removal of which has less severe consequences for readers' preferences. In other words, older literature may, in the course of time, become dependent on devices of foregrounding that have themselves become automatized because of readers' frequent exposure to them. Consequently, the literary communication process may itself be constantly prone to strong internal erosive powers: while the use of foregrounding devices should be the marking of the speech action pattern as a literary one, historical evolution may directly work against the employment of specific types of such marking: by 'signalling' literature by means of foregrounding devices, consumers of literature develop adaptive expectations towards these markings, thereby prohibiting any standardization process of the marking, or at least eroding its potential for activating pattern-knowledge required for the identification of literary forms of communication. Such an evolutionary account of foregrounding would also be supported by Martindale (1975).

It is this pragmatic analysis of the concept of FG, as elaborated in the previous paragraphs, that I consider as most promising for future work in stylistics. With regard to FG, older studies have often taken a naive essentialist position in this respect, leading to over-simplified notions of literariness or poeticality. Instead of adopting such a view it may be both more adequate and more rewarding for future research to consider FG as a relational and dynamic concept, embedded within the social and cultural constellation of a particular historical time. The present study has gone some way to outline such a general perspective on the theory, and to test some of its major assumptions. In order to further investigate the pragmatic nature of the notion of FG, it will be necessary to provide more detailed studies of the way in which particular pattern-knowledge and cultural values are activated by different types of foregrounding devices in the reading process.

BIBLIOGRAPHY

Anastasi, A. (ed.) (1966). Testing Problems in Perspective. Washington: Amer. Counc. on Educ.

Arnheim, R. (1954). Art and Visual Perception.

Arnheim, R. (1971). Entropy and Art: An Essay on Disorder and Order. Berkeley: University of California.

Austerlitz, R. (1961). 'Parallelismus'. In Davie, D. et al., (eds.). Poetics I. (1961: 439-444). Warsaw & The Hague: Mouton.

Austin, J.L. (1962). How to do Things with Words. Oxford: Oxford University Press.

Bann, S. & Bowlt, J.E. (eds.) (1973). Russian Formalism: A Collection of Articles and Texts in Translation. Edinburgh: Scottish Academic Press.

Beaugrande, R.A. de (1978). 'Information, Expectation, and Processing: On classifying Poetic Texts'. Poetics 7. 3-44.

Berlyne, D.E. (1974). Studies in the New Experimental Aesthetics. Washington: Hemisphere.

Carroll, J.B. (1960). 'Vectors of Prose Style'. In Sebeok (1960: 283-292).

Chafe, W.L. (1972). 'Discourse Structure and Human Knowledge'. In Carroll, J.B. & Freedle, R.D. (eds.). Language Comprehension and the Acquisition of Knowledge. (1972: 41-69). New York: Wiley.

Chapman, A.J. & Williams, A.R. (1976). 'Prestige Effects and Aesthetic Experiences: Adolescents' Reactions to Music'. British Journal of Social and Clinical Psychology 15. 61-72.

Child, D. (1970). The Essentials of Factor Analysis. London: Holt, Rinehart & Winston.

Chomsky, N. (1964). 'Degrees of Grammaticalness'. In Fodor & Katz (1964: 384-389).

Cluysenaar, A. (1976). Introduction to Literary Stylistics. London: Batsford.

Crystal, D. & Davy, D. (1969). Investigating English Style. London: Longman.

Culler, J. (1975). Structuralist Poetics. London: Routledge & Kegan Paul.

Cummings, E.E. (1960). Selected Poems. 1923-1958. London: Faber & Faber.

Dickinson, E. (1968). A choice of Emily Dickinson's Verse. (ed. Hughes, T.). London: Faber & Faber.

Dijk, T.A. van (1977). Text and Context. Explorations in the Semantics and Pragmatics of Discourse. London: Longman.

Dijk, T.A. van (1980). Macro-structures. An interdisciplinary Study of Global Structures in Discourse, Interaction, and Cognition. Hillsdale, N.J.: Lawrence Erlbaum.

Doležel, L. (1968). 'Russian and Prague School Functional Stylistics'. Style 2.2. 143-158.

Dorsch, T.S. (1965). Classical Literary Criticism. Harmondsworth: Penguin.

Duchastel, P.C. & Merrill, P.F. (1973). 'The effects of behavioral objectives on learning; a review of empirical studies'. Review of Educational Research 43. 53-69.

Ehlich, K. & Rehbein, J. (1980). 'Sprache in Institutionen'. In Althaus, H. P. et al. (eds.), Lexikon der germanistischen Linguistik (1980: 338-345). Tübingen: Max Niemeyer.

Eisenmann, R. & Boss, E. (1970). 'Complexity-simplicity and Persuasibility'. Perceptual and Motor Skills 31. 651-656.

Erlich, V. (1965). Russian Formalism: History-Doctrine. The Hague: Mouton.

Faw, H.W. & Waller, T.G. (1976). 'Mathemagenic behaviours and efficiency in learning from prose materials: review, critique and recommendations'. Review of Educational Research 46. 691-720.

Fish, S.E. (1970). 'Literature in the Reader: Affective Stylistics'. New Literary History 2. 123-162.

Fish, S.E. (1973). 'How Ordinary is Ordinary Language?'. New Literary History 5. 41-54.

Flaker, A. & Zmegač, V. (1974). Formalismus, Strukturalismus und Geschichte: zur Literaturtheorie und Methodologie in der Sowjet-Union, CSSR, Polen und Jugoslavien. Kronberg Ts: Scriptor.

Fodor, J.A. & Katz, J.J. (Eds.) (1964). The Structure of Language: Readings in the Philosophy of Language. Englewood Cliffs, N.J.: Prentice Hall.

Fokkema, D.W. (1976). 'Continuity and Change in Russian Formalism, Czech Structuralism, and Soviet Semiotics'. Poetics and Theory of Literature (PTL) 1. 153-196.

Fowler, R.G. (1971). The Languages of Literature. London: Routledge & Kegan Paul.

Fowler, R.G. (1984). 'Studying Literature as Language'. Dutch Quarterly Review of Anglo-American Letters 14. 171-184.

Freeman, D.C. (1970). Linguistics and Literary Style. New York: Holt, Rinehart & Winston, Inc.

Garvin, P. (1964). A Prague School Reader on Esthetics, Literary Structure and Style. Washington: Georgetown University Press.

Gimson, A.C. (1962). An Introduction to the Pronunciation of English. London: Arnold.

Gordon, I.E. & Gardner, C. (1974). 'Responses to altered pictures'. British Journal of Psychology 65. 243-251.

Groos, R.S. (1975). Foregrounding and Defamiliarization in the Rabelaisian Narrative. University of Wisconsin, Ph. D. Dissertation.

Halliday, M.A.K. (1971). 'Linguistic Function and Literary Style'. In Chatman, S. Literary Style: A Symposium. (1971: 330-368). London: Oxford University Press.

Hansson, G. (1964). Dikt i Profil. Göteborg: Gumperts.

Hawkes, T. (1977). Structuralism and Semiotics. London: Methuen.

Heise, D.R. (1969). 'Some Methodological Issues in Semantic Differential Research'. Psychological Bulletin 72. 406-422.

Jakobson, R. (1960). 'Closing Statement: Linguistics and Poetics'. In Sebeok (1960: 350-377).

Jakobson, R. (1966). 'Grammatical Parallelism and its Russian Facet'. Language 42. 399-429.

Jakobson, R. (1968). 'Poetry of Grammar and Grammar of Poetry'. Lingua 21. 597-609.

Jakobson, R. & Jones, L.G. (1970). Shakespeare's Verbal Art in 'Th' Expence of Spirit'. The Hague: Mouton.

Jakobson, R. & Lévi-Strauss, C. (1962). '"Les Chats" de Charles Baudelaire'. L'Homme 2. 5-21.

Jameson, F. (1972). The Prison-House of Language: A Critical Account of Structuralism and Russian Formalism. Princeton & London: Princeton University Press.

Katz, J.J. (1964). 'Semi-sentences'. In Fodor & Katz (1964: 400-416).

Keele, S.W. (1973). Attention and Human Performance. Pacific Palisades, California: Goodyear Co.

Kintgen, E.R. (1977). 'Reader Response and Stylistics'. Style 11. 1-18.

Konečni, V.J. & Sargent-Pollock, D. (1976). 'Choice between Melodies Differing in Complexity under Divided-Attention Conditions'. Journal of Experimental Psychology: Human Perception and Performance 2. 347-356.

Kreitler, H. & Kreitler, S. (1972). Psychology of the Arts. Durham, N.C.: Duke Press.

Kress, G. (ed.) (1976). Halliday: System and Function in Language. Oxford: Oxford University Press.

Leech, G.N. (1966). 'Linguistics and the Figures of Rhetoric'. In Fowler, R.G. Essays on Style and Language. (1966: 135-156). London: Routledge & Kegan Paul.

Leech, G.N. (1969). A Linguistic Guide to English Poetry. London: Longman.

Leech, G.N. (1970). '"This Bread I break" - Language and Interpretation'. In Freeman (1970: 119-128).

Leech, G.N. (1983). Principles of Pragmatics. London: Longman.

Lemon, L.T. & Reis, M. (1965). Russian Formalist Criticism: Four Essays. Lincoln: Nebraska University Press.

Levin, S.R. (1962). Linguistic Structures in Poetry. The Hague: Mouton.

Levin, S.R. (1963). 'Deviation - Statistical and Determinate - in Poetic Language'. Lingua 12. 276-290.

Levin, S.R. (1964). 'Poetry and Grammaticalness'. In Lunt, H.G. (ed.). Proceedings of the Ninth International Congress of Linguists. (1964: 308-315). The Hague: Mouton.

Levin, S.R. (1965). 'Internal and External Deviation in Poetry'. Word 21. 225-237.

Levinson, (1983). Pragmatics. Cambridge: Cambridge University Press.

Lindauer, M.S. (1974). The Psychological Study of Literature. Limitations, Possibilities, and Accomplishments. Chicago: Nelson Hall.

Lipski, J.M. (1977). 'Poetic Deviance and Generative Grammar'. Poetics and Theory of Literature (PTL) 2. 241-256.

Lotman, Y. (1976). Analysis of the Poetic Text. Ann Arbor: Ardis.

Martindale, C. (1973). 'Approximation to Natural Language, Grammaticalness, and Poeticality'. Poetics 9. 21-25.

Martindale, C. (1975). Romantic progression: the psychology of literary history. Washington, D.C.: Hemisphere.

Milic, L.T. (1969). Stylists on Style. New York: C. Scribner's Sons.

Miller, G.A. (1960). 'Closing Statement: From the Viewpoint of Psychology'. In Sebeok (1960: 386-395).

Miller, G.A. & Selfridge, J.A. (1950). 'Verbal Context and the Recall of Meaningful Material'. American Journal of Psychology 63. 176-185.

Moles, A. (1968). Information Theory and Esthetic Perception. Urbana, Ill.: University Press.

Moser, R.E. (1974). Foregrounding in the Sunjata, the Mande Epic. University of Indiana, Ph. D. Dissertation.

Mukařovský, J. (1964$_a$). 'Standard Language and Poetic Language'. In Garvin (1964: 17-30).

Mukařovský, J. (1964$_b$). 'The Esthetics of Language'. In Garvin (1964: 31-69).

Mukařovský, J. (1977). The Word and Verbal Art: Selected Essays. Yale: Yale University Press.

Nie, N., Bent, D.H. & Hull, C.H. (1970). Statistical Package for the Social Sciences. New York: McGraw Hill.

Noll, A.M. (1966). 'Human or Machine? A Subjective Comparison of Piet Mondrian's Composition with Lines (1917) with a Computer Generated Picture'. Psychological Record 16. 1-10.

O'Hare, D. (1976). 'Individual Differences in Perceived Similarity and Preference for Visual Art: A Multidimensional Scaling Analysis'. Perception and Psychophysics 20. 445-452.

Ohmann, R. (1971). 'Speech Acts and the Definition of Literature'. Philosophy and Rhetoric 4. 1-19.

Oppenheim, A.N. (1966). Questionnaire Design and Attitude Measurement. London: Heinemann.

Osgood, C.E., Suci, G.I. & Tannenbaum, P.H. (1957). The Measurement of Meaning. Urbana, Ill.: Illinois University Press.

O'Toole, L.M. & Shukman, A. (eds.) (1975-78). Russian Poetics in Translation. Vols. 1-5. Oxford: Holdan Books.

Bibliography

Peer, W. van (1980). The Stylistic Theory of Foregrounding: A Theoretical and Empirical Investigation. University of Lancaster, Ph. D. Dissertation.

Peer, W. van (1983). 'Poetic Style and Reader Response: An Exercise in Empirical Semics'. Journal of Literary Semantics 12. 2-16.

Peer, W. van (forthcoming). 'Top-down and Bottom-up: Interpretative Strategies in the Reading of E.E. Cummings'. New Literary History (forthcoming).

Pomorska, K. (1968). Russian Formalist Theory and its Poetic Ambiance. The Hague: Mouton.

Popper, K.R. (1972). Objective Knowledge. An Evolutionary Approach. Oxford: Clarendon Press.

Pratt, M.L. (1977). Toward a Speech Act Theory of Literary Discourse. Bloomington: Indiana University Press.

Raeff, L. (1955). The Effects of Poetic and Literal Orientations on the Meaning Structure of Words. Clark University, Worcester, Mass. Ph. D. Dissertation.

Riffaterre, M. (1959). 'Criteria for Style Analysis'. Word 15. 154-174.

Riffaterre, M. (1960). 'Stylistic Context'. Word 16. 207-218.

Riffaterre, M. (1964). 'The Stylistic Function'. In Lunt, H.G. (ed.). Proceedings of the Ninth International Congress of Linguists. (1964: 316-323). The Hague: Mouton.

Riffaterre, M. (1972). 'Describing Poetic Structures: Two Approaches to Baudelaire's "Les Chats"'. In Babb, H.S. Essays in Stylistic Analysis. (1972: 362-392). New York: Harcourt Brace Jovanovich, Inc.

Robson, C. (1973). Experiment, Design and Statistics in Psychology. Harmondsworth: Penguin.

Roethke, T. (1957). Words for the Wind. London: Secker & Warburg.

Rossetti, C. (1904). The Poetical Works of Christina Georgina Rossetti. (ed. Rossetti, W.M.). London: Macmillan.

Schmid, W. (1973). 'Poetische Sprache in formalistischer Sicht: Zu einer neuen Anthologie Russischer Formalisten'. Zeitschrift für Französische Sprache und Literatur 83. 260-271.

Searle, J.R. (1969). Speech Acts. Cambridge: Cambridge University Press.

Sebeok, T.A. (1960). Style in Language. Cambridge, Mass.: M.I.T. Press.

Shapiro, M. (1976). Asymmetry: An Enquiry into the Linguistic Structure of Poetry. Amsterdam: North Holland.

Short, M. (1973$_a$). 'Some Thoughts on Foregrounding and Interpretation'. Language and Style 6. 97-108.

Short, M. (1973$_b$). 'Linguistic Criticism and Baudelaire's "Les Chats"'. Journal of Literary Semantics 2. 79-93.

Siegel, S. (1956). Nonparametric Statistics for the Behavioral Sciences. London: McGraw-Hill.

Snider, J.G. & Osgood, C.E. (1969). Semantic Differential Technique. A Sourcebook. Chicago: Aldine.

Stankiewicz, E. (1960). 'Linguistics and the Study of Poetic Language'. In Sebeok (1960: 69-81).

Steck, L. & Machotka, P. (1975). 'Preference for Musical Complexity: Effect of Context'. Journal of Experimental Psychology 104. 170-174.

Thomas, D. (1971). Collected Poems. 1934-1952. New York: New Directions Books.

Thorne, J.P. (1970). 'Generative Grammar and Stylistic Analysis'. In Lyons, J. (ed.) New Horizons in Linguistics. (1970: 185-197). Harmondsworth: Penguin.

Valentine, C.W. (1962). The Experimental Psychology of Beauty. London: Methuen.

Vernon, M.D. (1975). The Psychology of Perception. Harmondsworth: Penguin.

Weinreich, U. (1972). Explorations in Semantic Theory. The Hague: Mouton.

Wellek, R. (1960). 'Closing Statement: From The Viewpoint of Literary Criticism'. In Sebeok (1960: 408-419).

Wellek, R. (1971). 'Stylistics, Poetics, and Criticism'. In Chatman, S. Literary Style: A Symposium. (1971: 65-76). London: Oxford University Press.

Wellek, R. & Warren, A. (1956). Theory of Literature. New York: Harcourt Brace Jovanovich, Inc.

Werth, P. (1976). 'Roman Jakobson's Verbal Analysis of Poetry'. Journal of Linguistics 12. 21-73.

Widdowson, H.G. (1972). 'On the Deviance of Literary Discourse'. Style 6. 294-308.

Widdowson, H.G. (1975). Stylistics and the Teaching of Literature. London: Longman.

Wordsworth, W. (1977). Poems. vol. 2. Harmondsworth: Penguin.

Ziff, P. (1964). 'On understanding "Understanding Utterances"'. In Fodor & Katz (1964: 390-399).

APPENDIX 1.

THE DATA COLLECTING INSTRUMENTS

ORAL INSTRUCTION

When Ss have taken their seats, read:

Welcome everybody. Before the experiment starts, make sure there is a pile of sheets in front of you. They should all be face down. If not, please tell me now.

Right then, will you now turn over the first sheet only. This should be 'Aims of the Project'. Please read the page completely. Now turn this sheet over and put it in the right hand corner of your table. Then turn over the next sheet. This is 'Part A'. Please complete the page carefully. Turn over this sheet as well and put it on top of the first one, in the right hand corner.

In the next part you will be given a poem to read. Read it through twice carefully. Then put the poem face down in the <u>left</u> hand corner of your table.

Now turn over the next page in front of you. This should be 'Part B'. Read the instructions carefully, and then complete this version of the poem. When ready, turn over this sheet and put it into the right hand corner, please.

Now pick up your poem, which is still in the left hand corner. Read it through again once only. Now please do the following: underline the words or phrases that struck you most when reading the poem, up to a maximum of ten words or phrases. When finished, put the poem face down in the right hand corner.

Turn over the next sheet now, which should be 'Part D'. Read the instructions carefully and carry them out. When finished, put 'Part D' face down in the right hand corner of your table.

Now turn over the following sheet, which will contain the poem again. Now pretend that you are English teachers working with 16-year old youngsters and assume all pupils understand all words in the poem. You want to give your pupils some idea of what poetry is about. Which part(s) of the poem would you then find especially worthy of comment, discussion, explanation, etc. Now please underline these passages that you would discuss with your pupils. When ready, turn over this copy of the poem as well and put it on top of the other sheets in the right hand corner.

(These instructions were repeated in the same form for the four poems used.)

PART A

Name:..
Major Subject:..
Table Number:...

In the table below you will find eight statements.
Circle the number you think appropriate for each
statement on a scale 1 to 5, with:

5 YES
4 SOMETIMES
3 NOT SURE
2 RARELY
1 NEVER

Circle one number only for each statement.
Do not spend long on this.

1) I like reading poetry.	5 4 3 2 1
2) I have studied poetry a lot.	5 4 3 2 1
3) I read a lot of poetry.	5 4 3 2 1
4) I find I understand poetry well.	5 4 3 2 1
5) I write poems myself.	5 4 3 2 1
6) It is important for society to have poets.	5 4 3 2 1
7) I study poetry a lot.	5 4 3 2 1
8) I find studying poetry interesting.	5 4 3 2 1

WHEN FINISHED PUT SHEET FACE DOWN IN RIGHT HAND CORNER

Appendix

PART B

Below you will find the text of the poem again. However some words
have been deleted and replaced by a dash. In those blanks you fill in the
precise words that are missing.
Be careful: fill in only one word in one blank!

    The Brain - is wider than the Sky -
    For - ------- them ------- by -------
    The one the other will -------
    With ------- - and You - beside -

    The ------- is deeper than the sea -
    For - hold them - Blue to Blue -
    The one the other will absorb -
    As Sponges - Buckets - do -

    The Brain is just the weight of God -
    For - Heft them - Pound for Pound -
    And they will differ - if they do -
    As ------- from Sound -

WHEN FINISHED, PUT THIS SHEET FACE DOWN IN THE RIGHT
HAND CORNER.

Appendix

Below you will find a list of 9 phrases from the poem.
Rank them in order of importance that they have in the poem, giving a
number 1 to the phrase you find the most important, and a number 9 to
the least important one.

unalterable pathos of basin
inexorable sadness of pencils
dropping a fine film
misery of manila folders
lonely reception room
endless duplication of lives
finer than flour
dolour of pad and paperweight
immaculate public places

WHEN FINISHED, PUT THIS SHEET FACE DOWN IN THE RIGHT
HAND CORNER.

PART F

INTRODUCTION

In reading a text people try to make sense of what is on a page: the printed words and sentences have to be interpreted in some way. Some parts however may be more important than others, and by looking carefully at these we can understand what is being communicated. In other words, in order to "get the message" a reader has to guess what is meant. But of course his guess must be consistent with the text itself. These "guesses" are what people mean when they talk about the interpretation of a poem.

In what follows we shall ask you to read a poem. Suppose a friend of yours comes along and asks you to explain what it is about. In that case you will give him/her your interpretation of what you have read. And perhaps you might like to draw his/her attention to certain parts of the text which you find important in arriving at its meaning.

Now this is exactly what we shall ask you to do next: indicate those parts in the poem that are especially important to arrive at your interpretation. Of course you will have to remember that your interpretation must account for as many important facts are possible in the text itself.

Appendix

PART G

INTRODUCTION

In the experiment we should like to find out in which way people react in reading poetic texts. There are no right or wrong answers in this test. We shall simply ask you to rate the qualities of various passages in the poems you have read. So please try to be as precise as you can about your own judgement.

Rating your reaction is done by circling the number that represents the degree of your opinion best. So the numbers on the scale may be expressed as follows:

1 EXTREMELY
2 VERY
3 RATHER
4 NEUTRAL
5 RATHER
6 VERY
7 EXTREMELY

Here is an example: how would you indicate that you find item X "very good" and "rather happy"? By circling the number 2 for "good" and the number 5 for "happy", in the following way:

| ITEM X | GOOD | | 1 2 3 4 5 6 7 BAD |
| | SAD | | 1 2 3 4 5 6 7 HAPPY |

The sheet for this task contains a set of line numbers, referring to the poem, and for each line number you will find five adjective pairs. You will be asked to rate each of these lines on each of the five adjective scales.

If you made a mistake you may correct it on the sheet, but make clear which is your final opinion.

Do not worry if some of the adjectives puzzle you. It is your intuitive response that we want. So fill in the scales as you "feel" the items should be judged. Also, do not linger too long on any one item. Try to provide a spontaneous reaction.

You may keep this sheet in front of you during the rating task.

Appendix

ADJECTIVAL SCALES

Line no. 1

POETIC	1 2 3 4 5 6 7	PROSAIC
INSIGNIFICANT	1 2 3 4 5 6 7	SIGNIFICANT
WORTHLESS	1 2 3 4 5 6 7	VALUABLE
SURPRISING	1 2 3 4 5 6 7	EXPECTED
DULL	1 2 3 4 5 6 7	EXCITING

Line no. 3

SURPRISING	1 2 3 4 5 6 7	EXPECTED
PROSAIC	1 2 3 4 5 6 7	POETIC
SIGNIFICANT	1 2 3 4 5 6 7	INSIGNIFICANT
DULL	1 2 3 4 5 6 7	EXCITING
VALUABLE	1 2 3 4 5 6 7	WORTHLESS

Line no. 6

EXCITING	1 2 3 4 5 6 7	DULL
SIGNIFICANT	1 2 3 4 5 6 7	INSIGNIFICANT
WORTHLESS	1 2 3 4 5 6 7	VALUABLE
PROSAIC	1 2 3 4 5 6 7	POETIC
SURPRISING	1 2 3 4 5 6 7	EXPECTED

Line no. 9

VALUABLE	1 2 3 4 5 6 7	WORTHLESS
EXPECTED	1 2 3 4 5 6 7	SURPRISING
EXCITING	1 2 3 4 5 6 7	DULL
PROSAIC	1 2 3 4 5 6 7	POETIC
SIGNIFICANT	1 2 3 4 5 6 7	INSIGNIFICANT

Line no. 10

WORTHLESS	1 2 3 4 5 6 7	VALUABLE
EXCITING	1 2 3 4 5 6 7	DULL
POETIC	1 2 3 4 5 6 7	PROSAIC
INSIGNIFICANT	1 2 3 4 5 6 7	SIGNIFICANT
EXPECTED	1 2 3 4 5 6 7	SURPRISING

Line 12

EXCITING	1 2 3 4 5 6 7	DULL
INSIGNIFICANT	1 2 3 4 5 6 7	SIGNIFICANT
PROSAIC	1 2 3 4 5 6 7	POETIC
VALUABLE	1 2 3 4 5 6 7	WORTHLESS
EXPECTED	1 2 3 4 5 6 7	SURPRISING

PART H

SMALL	1 2 3 4 5 6 7	LARGE
VALUABLE	1 2 3 4 5 6 7	WORTHLESS
SURPRISING	1 2 3 4 5 6 7	EXPECTED
DULL	1 2 3 4 5 6 7	EXCITING
COMPLEX	1 2 3 4 5 6 7	SIMPLE
INSIGNIFICANT	1 2 3 4 5 6 7	SIGNIFICANT
STRONG	1 2 3 4 5 6 7	WEAK
OLD	1 2 3 4 5 6 7	NEW
INTERESTING	1 2 3 4 5 6 7	BORING
USUAL	1 2 3 4 5 6 7	UNUSUAL
PASSIVE	1 2 3 4 5 6 7	ACTIVE
DEEP	1 2 3 4 5 6 7	SHALLOW
PROSAIC	1 2 3 4 5 6 7	POETIC

Appendix

ALTERED VERSION OF E. DICKINSON'S POEM

1   The Brain - is <u>vaster</u> than the Sky -
2   For - put them side by side -
3   The one the other will contain
4   With ease - and You - beside -

5   The Brain is deeper than the sea
6   For - hold them - Blue to Blue -
7   And <u>it will absorb the other one</u> -
8   As Sponges - Buckets - <u>will</u>

9   The Brain is just the weight of God -
10   For - Heft them - Pound for Pound -
11   And they will differ - if they do -
12   As Syllable from <u>Word</u> -

ALTERED VERSION OF T. ROETHKE'S POEM

DOLOUR
1   I have known the inexorable sadness of <u>people,</u>
2   Neat in their <u>offices, with piles of pads and paperweights,</u>
3   All the misery of manila folders and mucilage,
4   Desolation in immaculate public places,
5   Lonely reception room, lavatory, switchboard,
6   The unalterable pathos of basin and pitcher,
7   <u>Routine</u> of multigraph, paper-clip, comma,
8   Endless duplication of lives and objects.
9   And I have seei. dust from the walls of institutions,
10   Finer than flour, alive, more dangerous than silica,
11   Sift, almost invisible, through long afternoons of tedium,
12   Dropping a fine film on nails and delicate eyebrows,
13   Glazing the pale hair, the duplicate grey standard <u>forms.</u>

ALTERED VERSION OF C. ROSSETTI'S POEM

MIRAGE

1 The hope I dreamed of was a dream,

2 Asleep I was; and now I wake,

3 Exceeding tattered, old and worn,

4 For a dream's sake.

5 I hang my harp upon a tree,

6 A weeping willow in a lake;

7 And silently it hangs there, wrung and snapt,

8 For a dream's sake.

9 Lie still, lie still, my breaking heart;

10 The final hope let me forsake:

11 Life, and the world, and mine own self, are changed

12 For a dream's sake.

ALTERED VERSION OF D. THOMAS' POEM

WAS THERE A TIME

1 Was there a time when dancers with their fiddles

2 In children's circuses could stay their troubles?

3 There was a time they could cry over books,

4 But time has put an end to all of that.

5 Under the arc of the sky they are unsafe.

6 What's better known is safest in this life.

7 Under the starlight they who use both arms

8 Have cleanest hands, and, as the heartless ghost

9 Alone is cold, so the wise man sees best.

Appendix

<u>PART I</u>

------- IS A PLEASANT COUNTRY:
      a Mine   b Yes   c Norway   d Love   e This
IF'S WINTRY
(MY -------)
      a dear   b lovely   c word   d cold   e god
LET'S OPEN THE -------
      a door   b window   c sentence   d year   e clouds

BOTH IS THE VERY WEATHER
(NOT EITHER)
MY TREASURE,
WHEN VIOLETS APPEAR

------- IS A DEEPER SEASON
      a Spring   b Summer   c This   d Winter   e Love
THAN -------;
      a reason   b any   c spring   d hate   e ours
MY SWEET ONE
(AND APRIL'S WHERE WE'RE)

APPENDIX 2.

THE EMPIRICAL DATA

APPENDIX 2B. FREQUENCIES OF CORRECT RECALLS (Part B)

	FG	BG
Cummings	127	74
Dickinson	154	102
Roethke	156	62
Thomas	98	200

APPENDIX 2C. FREQUENCIES OF UNDERLINED WORDS (Part C)

	FG	BG
Cummings	497	135
Dickinson	336	274
Roethke	523	383
Thomas	509	356

APPENDIX 2D. RANK ORDERS ACCORDING TO "IMPORTANCE" (Part D)

CUMMINGS Line number	Mean rank allocated	DICKINSON Line number	Mean rank allocated	ROETHKE Line number	Mean rank allocated	THOMAS Line number	Mean rank allocated
1	3.5	2	5.0	1	1.8	2	6.4
2	5.5	2	6.8	2	4.1	2	5.2
3	10.0	3	5.4	3	3.6	3	5.0
4	5.7	5	2.8	4	4.1	4	2.8
5	4.8	6	4.3	5	4.5	5	5.2
6	8.8	7	3.0	6	4.3	6	4.0
7	9.8	9	1.3	8	1.0	7	4.2
8	7.8	10	5.2	10	7.0	8	2.2
9	2.2	12	2.5	12	5.7	9	1.1
10	6.0						
11	9.5						
12	4.8						

APPENDIX 2E. FREQUENCIES OF UNDERLINED WORDS (Part E)

	FG	BG
Cummings	556	169
Dickinson	645	356
Roethke	709	442
Thomas	605	443

APPENDIX 2F. FREQUENCIES OF UNDERLINED WORDS (Part F)

	FG	BG
Dickinson	686	432
Thomas	660	456
Wordsworth	488	361

APPENDIX 2F. RANK ORDERS ACCORDING TO 'IMPORTANCE' (Part F)

DICKINSON		THOMAS		WORDSWORTH	
Line number	Mean rank allocated	Line number	Mean rank allocated	Line number	Mean rank allocated
1	3.1	1	5.8	1	3.4
2	9.5	2	6.5	2	3.0
3	6.0	3	6.2	3	6.5
4	7.8	4	3.9	4	4.5
5	3.7	5	5.7	5	5.3
6	9.9	6	2.0	6	4.3
7	6.6	7	5.9	7	4.5
8	9.9	8	4.8	8	4.1
9	2.3	9	3.9		
10	8.1				
11	4.8				
12	5.2				

APPENDIX 2G. MEDIAN RATINGS ON SEMANTIC DIFFERENTIAL SCALES (Part G)

CUMMINGS

Line	Poetic	Significant	Valuable	Exciting	Surprising
1	4.4	4.9	4.7	4.5	6.3
3	4.5	5.3	4.8	4.2	4.9
7	4.3	4.4	4.1	4.3	4.6
8	4.4	4.3	4.8	3.8	3.0
9	6.1	6.6	6.3	5.8	4.0
12	5.5	5.9	5.5	5.0	4.4

ROETHKE

Line	Poetic	Significant	Valuable	Exciting	Surprising
1	3.5	5.4	5.4	4.5	6.1
4	4.2	5.4	5.8	4.8	5.0
5	4.4	5.4	5.3	2.6	3.9
8	4.8	5.7	6.1	4.7	4.6
10	5.6	5.1	5.5	5.3	5.4
13	5.6	5.7	5.6	5.1	3.6

ROSSETTI

Line	Poetic	Significant	Valuable	Exciting	Surprising
1	6.0	5.6	5.8	4.7	4.4
3	5.2	5.4	5.3	4.9	3.9
6	5.7	5.6	4.9	4.4	3.1
9	5.4	5.4	5.5	5.4	4.9
10	5.5	5.6	5.2	4.8	3.2
12	4.1	5.5	4.8	4.8	3.2

Appendix

APPENDIX 2H. MEDIAN RATINGS ON SEMANTIC DIFFERENTIAL SCALES (Part H)

The 13 columns represent the semantic differential scales, indicated by their numbers; their names are to be found on p. 134-135 and 159 of this study. Horizontal rows depict responses to lines in poems, numbered as follows:

	Original lines	Altered lines
Dickinson	1- 4	17-20
Roethke	5- 8	21-24
Rossetti	9-12	25-28
Thomas	13-16	29-32

Line	1	2	3	4	5	6	7	8	9	10	11	12	13
1	2.3	2.6	2.6	2.7	4.7	2.7	2.3	3.0	2.0	2.5	3.5	2.7	2.5
17	1.4	2.6	2.0	2.0	3.2	2.1	1.9	2.5	1.9	2.5	3.5	2.2	3.7
2	3.5	3.5	2.8	3.1	3.1	2.7	3.0	3.7	2.5	2.5	2.7	3.0	3.3
18	3.0	2.5	3.5	3.0	2.8	2.5	2.6	2.4	2.5	2.7	2.5	2.3	4.4
3	4.5	4.0	4.0	4.7	5.3	3.5	4.3	4.0	3.5	3.1	3.1	3.7	4.5
19	4.0	3.5	3.7	4.5	4.8	3.0	4.5	4.0	3.5	3.5	4.5	3.7	5.2
4	4.0	3.0	2.2	2.7	2.5	2.5	2.9	2.5	2.5	2.5	3.5	2.3	2.3
20	2.5	2.0	3.0	2.3	3.3	1.7	2.3	3.3	2.3	3.5	4.0	2.5	3.0
5	3.0	2.7	1.8	2.0	2.5	2.7	1.5	1.5	1.8	1.5	3.3	1.5	3.0
21	3.5	2.4	3.0	3.5	3.5	1.7	2.3	4.5	2.3	3.2	4.7	2.8	4.5
6	4.3	3.0	3.6	4.0	3.7	3.2	4.0	2.8	3.0	3.0	5.3	4.0	2.8
22	4.5	3.8	4.3	5.0	4.3	2.7	3.5	3.7	4.0	4.2	5.2	4.3	4.2
7	3.4	2.8	3.5	3.5	4.8	2.3	3.5	3.5	2.5	3.0	4.0	3.0	2.5
23	5.2	4.5	5.7	4.0	5.0	2.3	3.0	3.5	3.4	3.2	5.0	4.5	4.7
8	2.0	1.8	4.3	2.8	3.3	2.0	2.4	2.8	2.3	2.7	4.0	2.0	3.2
24	4.0	3.5	2.8	3.7	3.8	2.4	2.3	3.0	3.0	2.8	4.0	3.0	3.2

Appendix

9	4.0	3.5	5.2	4.0	5.7	1.5	4.0	5.5	4.0	5.5	5.3	4.0	3.0
25	3.7	3.5	5.3	4.3	5.4	2.3	3.7	5.7	3.7	5.1	5.2	4.5	2.9
10	3.5	3.5	4.5	3.3	5.5	2.5	4.5	4.5	3.5	4.7	5.0	5.3	3.0
26	3.5	3.5	2.8	3.5	4.4	2.5	2.7	3.5	2.5	3.5	4.5	3.0	2.5
11	3.5	2.7	2.5	2.5	3.5	2.5	3.0	4.5	2.5	2.3	2.5	2.0	1.7
27	3.6	2.8	3.3	3.0	3.1	2.6	2.4	4.4	2.7	2.5	5.5	2.9	2.5
12	3.5	3.5	5.3	4.5	5.5	3.3	4.0	5.5	4.0	5.3	5.5	4.5	2.5
28	2.6	2.5	3.6	3.5	4.5	2.3	2.8	5.4	3.2	4.5	5.2	3.1	2.7
13	3.5	2.7	3.6	2.5	3.3	1.8	2.3	4.3	2.8	2.8	2.5	2.5	2.5
29	3.5	2.8	4.0	4.0	5.5	2.5	4.5	4.5	3.7	4.8	4.0	2.5	4.7
14	3.3	2.4	3.0	3.2	2.7	2.1	2.7	4.7	2.7	3.5	4.8	2.0	4.8
30	4.4	3.3	5.0	5.0	5.3	3.0	4.8	4.5	4.5	4.8	5.5	4.5	5.3
15	3.1	3.5	2.3	3.0	2.3	2.5	2.3	2.5	2.1	2.5	4.9	2.3	3.0
31	3.5	3.5	2.4	3.7	2.6	3.5	3.0	2.5	3.5	2.5	2.8	2.7	3.0
16	2.7	2.1	2.7	3.2	2.8	1.8	2.5	4.4	2.3	3.1	4.3	2.3	3.2
32	3.5	2.9	3.3	3.5	2.8	2.5	3.5	3.0	4.0	2.7	4.5	3.0	3.0

Appendix

FACTOR ANALYSIS OF ORIGINAL LINES

VARIABLE	EST	COMMUNALITY	FACTOR	EIGENVALUE	PCT OF VAR	CUM PCT
SMALL		1.00000	1	6.29751	48.4	48.4
VAL		1.00000	2	1.33536	10.3	58.7
SUR		1.00000	3	1.00803	7.8	66.5
DULL		1.00000	4	.76232	5.9	72.3
COM		1.00000	5	.66508	5.1	77.4
INSIG		1.00000	6	.60024	4.6	82.1
STRO		1.00000	7	.51335	3.9	86.0
OLD		1.00000	8	.42148	3.2	89.3
INT		1.00000	9	.35562	2.7	92.0
USU		1.00000	10	.32202	2.5	94.5
PASS		1.00000	11	.25492	2.0	96.4
DEEP		1.00000	12	.23721	1.8	98.3
PROS		1.00000	13	.22686	1.7	100.0

FACTOR MATRIX USING PRINCIPAL FACTOR, NO ITERATIONS

	FACTOR 1	FACTOR 2	FACTOR 3	FACTOR 4	FACTOR 5	FACTOR 6
SMALL	-.64213	.39557	-.22269	.17003	.41794	.04057
VAL	.73834	-.36861	.01548	-.23573	.23797	-.00549
SUR	.64555	.47896	.13309	.07472	.36905	.02507
DULL	-.80978	.18304	-.01981	-.04148	.01280	.11064
COM	.57999	.31358	.35583	.26469	-.20978	.53305
INSIG	-.76962	.31117	-.01287	-.01803	-.24296	-.03879
STRO	.79781	-.18437	.06162	.07473	-.18352	-.04157
OLD	-.53430	-.55016	.11937	.40785	.32753	.15775
INT	.84416	-.03210	.07253	-.04560	.13427	-.04912
USU	-.69767	-.49176	.02512	.10260	-.08668	.20047
PASS	-.53194	-.03317	.48961	-.59574	.16309	.22750
DEEP	.85349	-.03979	.10748	.10224	.03465	-.00910
PROS	-.45401	.05226	.73355	.22420	-.00938	-.42307

VARIMAX ROTATED FACTOR MATRIX
AFTER ROTATION WITH KAISER NORMALIZATION

	FACTOR 1	FACTOR 2	FACTOR 3	FACTOR 4	FACTOR 5	FACTOR 6
SMALL	-.78604	.25841	.02268	.30104	-.21449	-.04301
VAL	.82479	-.02867	.06228	.22240	-.06074	-.23526
SUR	.25199	-.24565	-.09024	.77517	.26929	-.02934
DULL	-.74231	.17289	.25980	-.18847	-.11898	.07541
COM	.24037	-.13870	-.06552	.23482	.90667	-.03226
INSIG	-.77520	-.06955	.12144	-.29180	-.07536	.19701
STRO	.72527	-.20889	-.27782	.05644	.24976	-.05377
OLD	-.14380	.89979	.04983	-.17977	-.11800	.14792
INT	.70306	-.21853	-.13336	.38354	.15149	-.10738
USU	-.29605	.57531	.18767	-.56476	-.11058	.04888
PASS	-.23052	.08472	.92390	-.11517	-.06108	.16167
DEEP	.69386	-.17679	-.23741	.32313	.27704	-.05559
PROS	-.21238	.15085	.16045	-.03410	-.03238	.93834

FACTOR ANALYSIS OF ALTERED LINES

VARIABLE	EST COMMUNALITY	FACTOR	EIGENVALUE	PCT OF VAR	CUM PCT
SMALL	1.00000	1	5.41947	41.7	41.7
VAL	1.00000	2	1.66897	12.8	54.5
SUR	1.00000	3	.97588	7.5	62.0
DULL	1.00000	4	.82314	6.3	68.4
COM	1.00000	5	.80996	6.2	74.6
INSIG	1.00000	6	.59960	4.6	79.2
STRO	1.00000	7	.54898	4.2	83.4
OLD	1.00000	8	.43434	3.3	86.8
INT	1.00000	9	.41849	3.2	90.0
USU	1.00000	10	.40747	3.1	93.1
PASS	1.00000	11	.35372	2.7	95.8
DEEP	1.00000	12	.27631	2.1	98.0
PROS	1.00000	13	.26367	2.0	100.0

FACTOR MATRIX USING PRINCIPAL FACTOR, NO ITERATIONS

	FACTOR 1	FACTOR 2	FACTOR 3	FACTOR 4	FACTOR 5	FACTOR 6
SMALL	.56593	-.30140	-.26519	-.54720	.29860	.15465
VAL	-.58699	.55159	-.11758	.26948	.06811	-.16692
SUR	-.61533	-.38389	.03349	.25673	.29778	.15351
DULL	.80641	-.19327	-.03183	-.01483	.11591	-.19326
COM	-.57086	-.51099	.32993	.14560	.12952	.14829
INSIG	.65268	-.33100	.27326	.27538	-.29423	.09231
STRO	-.74839	.28663	-.02930	-.09127	.02807	-.10040
OLD	.57620	.47112	.25957	.04337	.14164	.48683
INT	-.77295	.26187	-.03178	-.24178	.15914	.14728
USU	.63437	.52624	-.03950	.08570	-.11502	.22440
PASS	.47464	.23910	.57018	.01747	.55975	-.27872
DEEP	-.79610	-.08529	.00555	.02327	.09223	.23756
PROS	.47202	-.06656	-.59510	.45943	.35982	.05607

VARIMAX ROTATED FACTOR MATRIX
AFTER ROTATION WITH KAISER NORMALIZATION

	FACTOR 1	FACTOR 2	FACTOR 3	FACTOR 4	FACTOR 5	FACTOR 6
SMALL	-.16093	-.17911	.89575	.16274	.04670	.07038
VAL	.63016	-.01691	-.59914	.09879	-.03947	.00887
SUR	.21865	.77165	-.11222	.11209	-.17647	-.07560
DULL	-.57418	-.33974	.35489	.26121	-.00098	.31682
COM	.01929	.81832	-.08894	-.20884	-.18061	-.04062
INSIG	-.86226	-.05637	.01555	-.00282	.18384	.02124
STRO	.67923	.15532	-.30593	-.20364	-.18172	-.09342
OLD	-.14952	-.24915	.08576	.04215	.85399	.23960
INT	.78650	.27581	-.09206	-.22719	-.01278	-.13271
USU	-.19104	-.57198	-.03033	.16187	.59813	.05741
PASS	-.14137	-.11918	.05492	.00740	.22123	.93201
DEEP	.50344	.57825	-.16309	-.13615	-.07773	-.25992
PROS	-.19888	-.10551	.11543	.92353	.08923	.01375

Appendix

APPENDIX 2 I. 'MULTIPLE CHOICE' RESULTS: EXPERIMENT (Part I)

CUMMINGS

		FG lines	BG lines
Poet	Originals	15	20
	Distractors	45	40
Scholar	Originals	18	24
	Distractors	66	60
Total	Originals	33	44
	Distractors	111	100

WORDSWORTH

		FG lines	BG lines
Poet	Originals	32	27
	Distractors	28	33
Scholar	Originals	42	42
	Distractors	42	42
Total	Originals	74	69
	Distractors	70	75

APPENDIX 2J. 'MULTIPLE CHOICE' RESULTS: QUESTIONNAIRE (Part J)

ROETHKE

		FG lines	BG lines
Poet	Originals	48	21
	Distractors	66	93
Scholar	Originals	42	39
	Distractors	108	111
Not indicated	Originals	146	138
	Distractors	214	222
Total	Originals	236	204
	Distractors	388	420

THOMAS

		FG lines	BG lines
Poet	Originals	20	3
	Distractors	100	117
Scholar	Originals	48	6
	Distractors	102	144
Not Indicated	Originals	90	3
	Distractors	270	357
Total	Originals	158	12
	Distractors	470	618

Appendix

APPENDIX 3.   REGRESSION MATRIX

Line no	X_1	X_2	X_3	X_4	X_5	X_6	X_7	X_8	X_9	X_{10}	X_{11}	Y_1	Y_2	Y_3	Y_4
1	8	9	10	8	1	1	0	8	0	2	0	47	31	40	118
2	7	8	8	4	0	1	0	5	0	2	2	25	18	16	59
3	3	0	0	2	0	0	0	3	0	0	0	2	2	1	5
4	6	3	6	0	0	0	0	5	0	2	0	19	17	17	53
5	6	3	7	9	1	1	0	6	0	2	0	35	24	38	97
6	2	0	2	1	0	1	1	3	0	1	0	6	4	1	11
7	2	0	0	2	0	0	0	2	0	0	0	3	1	1	5
8	4	0	0	3	0	0	1	2	0	0	1	9	9	8	26
9	7	10	10	8	0	0	2	6	0	4	1	42	32	46	120
10	2	0	2	2	0	0	0	1	0	1	0	10	10	10	30
11	2	4	6	2	0	0	0	3	0	0	0	2	2	1	5
12	2	10	9	5	0	0	2	5	0	2	2	38	31	34	103
13	7	4	4	10	0	0	0	9	0	3	0	32	28	38	98
14	6	5	7	10	0	0	0	4	0	1	0	0	0	0	0
15	6	4	5	9	1	0	0	6	0	1	0	12	12	21	45
16	5	3	3	0	0	0	0	1	0	0	1	10	8	22	40
17	8	4	4	10	0	0	0	10	0	3	0	17	11	8	36
18	8	16	12	10	0	0	0	4	0	2	0	9	5	7	21
19	4	8	0	9	1	0	0	6	0	1	0	8	10	24	42
20	7	8	5	3	1	1	1	3	0	0	0	22	21	27	68
21	10	17	17	10	0	0	2	8	0	5	4	32	24	21	77
22	9	16	18	10	0	0	0	4	1	1	0	30	17	12	58
23	4	11	5	10	0	0	2	7	1	2	1	7	12	7	26
24	5	0	6	3	0	0	1	4	1	2	2	33	29	37	99
25	11	22	22	5	0	0	0	7	0	2	0	38	28	37	103
26	9	9	8	4	0	0	1	10	1	2	0	23	12	18	53
27	9	21	21	5	0	0	0	9	1	2	0	33	24	23	80
28	7	12	6	3	1	0	0	4	1	0	0	16	20	33	69
29	10	5	5	3	1	0	0	4	1	0	0	4	8	8	20
30	8	0	0	2	0	0	0	8	2	2	2	23	24	22	69

31	8	5	6	5	0	0	0	7	1	2	4	12	9	9	30
32	6	4	0	4	0	0	1	9	0	2	4	44	15	35	94
33	10	18	13	7	0	0	2	5	0	1	3	12	13	15	40
34	10	11	0	6	0	0	1	5	2	1	2	21	27	22	70
35	12	24	14	4	0	0	1	2	1	3	0	16	27	24	66
36	12	13	1	4	0	0	1	6	0	1	2	27	16	15	59
37	11	19	20	8	1	0	1	10	5	5	3	58	46	45	153
38	5	5	6	6	0	0	0	11	0	0	0	17	11	12	40
39	8	8	3	6	1	0	0	7	1	0	0	12	12	13	37
40	4	14	0	6	1	0	0	8	0	0	0	16	23	20	59
41	9	16	16	9	0	0	2	7	2	5	5	34	38	34	106
42	10	18	0	10	0	0	1	8	0	2	3	23	16	31	70
43	7	15	9	11	0	0	0	8	0	0	0	54	41	55	150
44	9	12	5	10	0	0	0	8	0	2	1	30	16	31	77
45	10	27	14	10	0	0	0	9	0	1	1	45	25	38	108
46	7	26	10	12	0	0	1	11	0	3	2	74	63	81	218